FIND OUT ABOUT

ANCIENT INDIA

What life was like for the ancient Indians

Daud Ali

CONSULTANT – Nick Allen

southwater

This edition is published by Southwater

Southwater is an imprint of Anness Publishing Ltd
Hermes House, 88–89 Blackfriars Road, London SE1 8HA
tel. 020 7401 2077; fax 020 7633 9499
www.southwaterbooks.com; info@anness.com

© Anness Publishing Ltd2000, 2003

This edition distributed in the UK by
The Manning Partnership Ltd,
6 The Old Dairy, Melcombe Road, Bath BA2 3LR;
tel. 01225 478 444; fax 01225 478 440;
sales@manning-partnership.co.uk

This edition distributed in the USA and Canada by
National Book Network,
4720 Boston Way, Lanham, MD 20706;
tel. 301 459 3366; fax 301 459 1705; www.nbnbooks.com

This edition distributed in Australia by Pan Macmillan
Australia, Level 18, St Martins Tower, 31 Market St,
Sydney, NSW 2000; tel. 1300 135 113; fax 1300 135 103;
customer.service@macmillan.com.au

This edition distributed in New Zealand by The Five Mile
Press (NZ) Ltd, PO Box 33–1071 Takapuna,
Unit 11/101–111 Diana Drive, Glenfield, Auckland 10;
tel. (09) 444 4144; fax (09) 444 4518; fivemilenz@clear.net.nz

Publisher: Joanna Lorenz
Managing Editor, Children's Books: Gilly Cameron Cooper
Editors: Joanne Hanks, Louisa Somerville, Edel Brosnan
Copy Editor: Gill Harvey
Designer: Caroline Reeves
Illustration: Stuart Carter, Chris Forsey, Rob Sheffield,
Clive Spong
Photography: John Freeman
Stylist: Melanie Williams
Reader: Jonathan Marshall
Production Controller: Yolande Denny

Anness Publishing would like to thank the following children for
modelling for this book:Emma Franklin, Samara Edwards-Amos,
Louis Jade, Adam Keevash, Christina Malcolm-Hansen, Ivelin
Nedkova, Thaddius Rivett, Luke Stanton

Previously published as *Step into Ancient India*

PICTURE CREDITS

B = bottom, t = top, c = centre, l = left, r = right

AKG: 9tr, 16tr, 16cl, 31tl, 33br, 34bl, 40tl, 46cr, 47cr, 47tr,
47cr, 51br, 54cl, 56c, 57tl, 51br, back cover, front cover; The
Ancient Art and Architechture Collection Ltd: 5ct, 14t, 14b
15tr, 20bl, 34br, 34tl, 44bl; 50br, front cover; The
Bridgeman Art Library : 4tr, 5tl, 11c, 11tl, 15bl, 17tl, 17tr,
17c, 18cl, 19c, 19tr, 19cl, 20tr, 21tl, 22tr, 27c, 29tr, 28cl,
31c, 32tl, 33tl, 33tr, 33bl, 35tl, 35cr, 36tl, 37tl, 40cr, 41tr,
43tl, 43tr, 43cl, 46tl, 46cl, 48tl, 49tl, 51tr, 51cl, 53c, 55tl,
54b, 58cr, 59tl, 59c, 60cr, 60cl, 61tr, title page; back cover;
Corbis: 2t, 3bl, 4cl, 15br, 21br, 28tl, 38tr, 44br, 45b, 55tr,
56tl, 57cl, 58tl, 60tl; C M Dixon: 3tr, 8tl, 10c, 44tl, back
cover; E T Archive: 9c, 10tr, 26tl, 29tl, 43bl,45tl, 47cl,
52cr, 53tr, 52tl, 55cr; Mary Evans Picture Library; 25bl,
26c; FLPA: 37c; Robert Harding: 24b, 25tr, 35br, 38b,
39bl, 42tl, 55b; The Hutchison library: 15tl, 23tr, 25tl,
42bl, 48cr, 59tr; Images of India: 20br, 22b, 21tr, 22b,
41tl, 41cl, 41c, 61cl; Philadelphia Museum of Art: 18tl;
Ann and Bury Peerless: 9tl, 45c; Link Picture Library: 5c,
23br; V & A Picture Library:12t, 23bl, 24t, 29c, 30tl,
30cl, 37tl, 49cl; Oxford Scientific Films: 35bl; Royal
Asiatic Society: 49c; Tony Stone Images: 15c, 23 tl, 27t.

10 9 8 7 6 5 4 3 2 1

CONTENTS

The Glory of Ancient India

THE INDIAN SUBCONTINENT IS HOME to one of the world's most ancient and varied civilizations. Many different groups of people have traveled over the Himalayan mountains and settled there. From the arrival of Aryan tribes about 3,000 years ago until the invasion of the Mughals in the 1500s, each new wave of people brought fresh ideas and ways of life. As a result, India's religious and artistic life became very rich and mixed.

Two major world religions—Hinduism and Buddhism—developed in ancient India, and for hundreds of years, India was also at the heart of Muslim life in Asia. These three religions shaped the course of India's history, and led to the building of magnificent monuments, many of which still stand.

With its Hindu and Buddhist temples and sculptures, and the sumptuous palaces of the Muslim rulers, India is full of amazing treasures from the past.

DAWN OF INDIAN CIVILIZATION
Ancient stone buildings, such as the Great Bath at Mohenjo-Daro in the Indus Valley, tell archaeologists a great deal about the dawn of civilization in India. Few buildings from later times have been excavated, partly because later houses were made of mud, thatch, and wood, none of which have survived.

BEAUTY IN STONE
A beautiful carving of a Yakshi (tree spirit) from Bharhut in central India. It is made of red sandstone, and dates back to 100 B.C. This Buddhist sculpture has a distinctive Indian style that you can see in sculptures from later eras. Buddhism was the first religion in India to inspire people to build monuments and make sculptures.

TIMELINE 6000 B.C.– A.D. 400

From early times until the coming of the British in 1757, India was divided into many kingdoms. It was never a single state. The regions of Ancient India were linked by a common culture, rather than by politics, religion, or language.

c. 6000 B.C. Neolithic settlements in Baluchistan.

c. 2800–2600 B.C. Beginnings of settlements in the Indus Valley region.

statue of priest king from Indus valley

rice cultivation

c. 2300–1700 B.C. Great cities of the Indus Valley (Mohenjo-Daro and Harappa), the Punjab (Kalibangan), and Gujarat (Lothal) flourished.

c. 1700 B.C. Sudden and mysterious decline of the Indus Valley civilization.

c. 1500–1200 B.C. Immigration of Vedic Aryans into northwestern India.

c. 1200–600 B.C. Vedic texts are composed.

c. 800 B.C. Use of iron for weapons and the spread of Aryan culture into the Gangetic plains.

c. 500–300 B.C. Rice cultivation and the introduction of iron for the use of agriculture in the eastern Gangetic plains lead to the formation of more complex societies, cities, and states.

fragment of pot with brahmi inscription

6000 B.C.   2500 B.C.   1200 B.C.   500 B.

TEMPLE OF THE SUN
A huge carved stone wheel forms a panel on the wall of the Sun Temple at Konarak on India's east coast. This part of the temple is carved in the shape of a gigantic twelve-wheeled chariot, drawn by seven stone horses. It dates back to the 1200s, when medieval Hindu kings built magnificent temples to their gods.

GRAND ENTRANCE
The Alamgiri Gate is one of three magnificent entrances built by the Mughal emperor Aurangzeb to the Shahadra fort at Lahore (in modern Pakistan). The fort doubled as a luxurious palace.

LIFE STORY
A limestone frieze that dates back to A.D. 100 shows a good deed performed by the spiritual leader, Buddha. The frieze comes from Amaravati, in southeastern India, which was an important Buddhist site after 300 B.C. Stories of the Buddha's past lives, called jatakas, were popular in ancient India.

A COUNTRY OF MOUNTAINS AND PLAINS
The Himalayan moutains form India's northern border, and the central Deccan plateau is framed by mountain ranges called the Eastern and Western Ghats. The first settlements grew up near rivers on the fertile plains in the north.

Map labels: R. Indus, HIMALAYAS, Mohenjo Daro, Delhi, River Ganges, Agra, R. Jamuna, Patiliputra, Broach, DECCAN PLATEAU, WESTERN GHATS, EASTERN GHATS, Kanchi, SRI LANKA

---

c. 500–400 B.C. Inscribed fragments of pots from Sri Lanka discovered.

c. 478–400 B.C. Life of the Buddha. He is born a prince but leaves his family to live in poverty.

327–325 B.C. Alexander the Great arrives in northwestern India.

coin of Alexander the Great

320 B.C. The rise of the Magadhan empire under the Maurya family, founded by King Chandragupta I.

268–233 B.C. King Ashoka, the grandson of Chandragupta I, issues the first royal edicts on pillars and rocks throughout the subcontinent.

c. 50 B.C.–A.D. 100 Intensive trade connections with the Roman Empire.

A.D. 50–A.D. 200 Kushanas and Shakas (tribes from Central Asia) set up kingdoms and adopt Indian religions. Indian dynasty of Satavahanas arises in southern India.

Ashokan pillar

c. A.D. 150 Kushana and Shaka kings in the north and west adopt Sanskrit as the courtly language.

c. A.D. 200–400 *Ramayana*, *Mahabharata* and the *Bhagavad-Gita* Hindu epic poems are composed in their final form.

A.D. 400 Almost all courts are using Sanskrit.

gateway to Buddhist stupa

300 B.C.　　　　A.D. 100　　　　A.D. 400

The Land of Ancient India

INDIA IS ISOLATED FROM THE main continent of Asia by the world's highest mountains, the Himalayas. The mountains made it difficult for people to invade. The easiest overland route, taken by the earliest settlers from Asia, is through the Karakoram mountains in the northwest (in present-day Afghanistan). Although these mountains are relatively low, it was still a difficult journey. Once people had arrived in India, they tended to stay.

The first people settled in the bare mountain foothills, and survived by keeping herds of animals, such as sheep and goats. People gradually moved south of the Himalayas, to areas where mighty rivers run through huge, fertile plains. Here, the climate enabled them to grow various crops.

India's climate is dominated by the monsoon, a wind that brings alternating seasons of hot, dry weather and heavy rain and flooding. In the drier west and north, wheat was the main crop from very early times, and higher rainfall in the east and south was ideal for growing rice. Rice cultivation was so successful in the plains around the Ganges river that many people settled there. This led to the growth of cities from 300 B.C. Later, cities developed along rivers further south.

From the first century A.D., people no longer needed to make the overland journey into India. They came by ship from as far away as the Mediterranean Sea, to ports on the west coast, in search of trade.

Tyre

ARABI

TRADING NATION
From 200 B.C., ancient India traded with the outside world by sea. They also bought and sold goods by land along the Silk Road—a route that cut across the Himalayas and through Central Asia, to Samarkand and beyond.

TIMELINE A.D. 250–1210

c. A.D. 250–1100 Many of the Hindu myths are written down in the literature called the *Puranas*.

c. A.D. 300 Bengal and South India develop trade and cultural contacts with Southeast Asia, which takes on many Indian cultural characteristics, building temples and monasteries, and adopting Sanskrit.

Chinese Buddhist monk

boar sculpture at Eran

c. A.D. 335–415 The Gupta empire is founded by a second king named Chandragupta I. He tries to establish a continental-wide empire.

c. A.D. 450–520 Huns attack and disrupt the Gupta empire and establish their own short-lived empire. They take on Indian ways, but their empire ends within a century, leaving a power vacuum in northern India.

c. A.D. 450–1200 Period of agricultural expansion throughout India. Tribal communities are forced to work as peasants on estates owned by brahmins and state officials. A feudal-like system emerges, with many regional empires relying on the vast farmlands for taxes.

c. A.D. 500–700 First Hindu temples constructed at Sanchi, Aihole, and Pattadakal.

monument from Borobodur

A.D. 250   A.D. 330   A.D. 500   A.D. 600

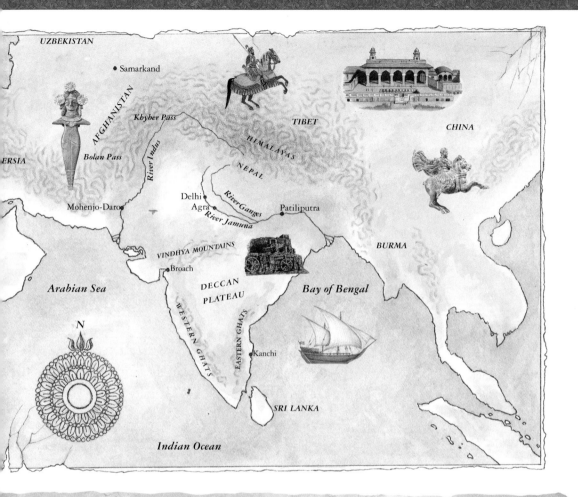

UZBEKISTAN

• Samarkand

AFGHANISTAN

Khyber Pass

Bolan Pass

PERSIA

River Indus

TIBET

HIMALAYAS

NEPAL

CHINA

Delhi
Agra

River Ganges

Patiliputra

River Jamuna

Mohenjo-Daro

BURMA

VINDHYA MOUNTAINS

• Broach

DECCAN
PLATEAU

Arabian Sea

Bay of Bengal

N

WESTERN GHATS

EASTERN GHATS

Kanchi

SRI LANKA

Indian Ocean

A.D. 606–647
Harshavardhana, king of
Kanauj, visited by
Hsiuen-tsang. Splendors
of courtly life and
medieval culture
flourish.

c. A.D. 630-643 The Chinese
monk, Hsiuen-tsang,
visits India to find
Buddhism in decline
in some areas.

*Krishna dancing
on serpent*

c. A.D. 712 Arab conquest of Sind by
Muhammad Ibn Qasim after the local king
refused to punish pirates who had
abducted a shipful of orphans
sent by the king of Sri Lanka to Baghdad.

c. A.D. 752 King
Dantidurga establishes a
powerful empire in
the Deccan, which is
recognized by Arab
geographers and
travelers as one of the
most powerful
kingdoms in Asia.

Kailasanath temple at Ilora

A.D. 997-1030 Sultan
Mahmud of Ghazni
makes 17 raids into
northern India to loot
temples of their
wealth.

copper-plate inscription

c. A.D. 1077 Embassy of merchants from
the Chola dynasty of southern India
arrive at the Sung court in China.

A.D. 1206 Aibak establishes the
Sultanate in Delhi, the
first Muslim kingdom in India.

A.D. 700

A.D. 900

A.D. 1210

History Makers

AN INFLUENTIAL LEADER
A statue of Gautama Buddha seated on a lotus flower. He founded Buddhism, which shaped life in India for thousands of years. Buddhism eventually died out in India, but it spread through many other parts of Asia. This created a link between India and many different eastern peoples and cultures.

MANY OF THE REMARKABLE FIGURES of Indian history who shaped the country's destiny were great leaders. Ashoka was a powerful ruler in the third century B.C., who encouraged the spread of Buddhism. Babur, a warlord from Samarkand in Central Asia, founded the Mughal Empire in India in the early 1500s. His grandson, Akbar, was a gifted politician and soldier who ruled for 49 years. The Mughal period was a time of huge development in the arts. Some Mughal rulers built magnificent cities, and many of their fine monuments and royal tombs can still be seen today.

From the time of the ancient civilization of the Aryans in the Indus Valley, religious teachers and scholars were respected. This may be because poverty and suffering have always been problems in India, which led people to think about why life was so difficult, and to seek ways of dealing with it. Two of the most famous religious leaders are Gautama Buddha, who established the Buddhist way of life, and Guru Nanak, who founded the Sikh religion.

TIMELINE A.D. 1290-1875

A.D. 1293 Marco Polo visits southern India. A flourishing trade is conducted throughout the Indian Ocean in silks, fabrics, spices, and other luxuries.

A.D. 1334-1370 The sultanate of Madurai, the southernmost Muslim kingdoms, established briefly in southern India before being defeated by southern kingdoms.

stone chariot from Vijayanagar

c. A.D. 1346–1565 Vijayanagar empire, the last great Hindu empire, founded in southern India.

c. A.D. 1360 Vedic and Hindu revival by the brothers Sayana and Madhava at the Vijayanagar court.

A.D. 1398 The Mongol Timur devastates Delhi.

tomb from the Sultanate period

c. A.D. 1440 Death of the Bhakti saint Kabir at Gorakhpur, where both Hindus and Muslims claim him as a great teacher.

A.D. 1469-1539 Life of Guru Nanak, founder of Sikhism.

A.D. 1498 Portuguese explorer, Vasco da Gama, visits Calicut.

A.D. 1510 The Portuguese conquer Goa.

Quth Minar marble fountain

A.D. 1290   A.D. 1340   A.D. 1400   A.D. 1520

8

ROYAL HANDWRITING

This signature of Emperor Harsha (A.D. 606–647) is carved in copper. Harsha was a patron (supporter) of arts and literature, and during his reign, the richness and elegance of the court reached new heights.

A SAINTLY LIFE

A statuette of Karaikal Ammaiyar, a woman who lived in southern India around A.D. 600. She was so devoted to the god Shiva that she left her home and family, and gave her life entirely to him. She fasted as a symbol of her faith and became incredibly thin. Karaikal Ammaiyar is revered as a saint even today in southern India.

ART LOVER

Shah Jahan was one of the greatest statesmen of the Mughal Empire. He extended Mughal power south into the Deccan plateau and north into Afghanistan. However, he did not fulfill the Mughal dream of capturing the trading city of Samarkand, the "blue pearl of the Orient," in Central Asia. Shah Jahan was a great patron of architecture.

ASHOKA'S PILLAR

An edict (order) of Ashoka, the ruler of India's first empire, is inscribed on this pillar. He published his edicts on pillars and rock faces throughout the land. Ashoka was a Buddhist. He claimed to have improved the lives of humans and animals, and helped to spread justice.

A.D. 1526 Babur, the Mongol, defeats the Sultan of Delhi and founds the Mughal empire.

A.D. 1556–1605 The reign of Akbar, the most enlightened Mughal emperor.

A.D. 1739 Nadir Shah sacks Delhi and carries off the Peacock Throne.

Mongol horseman

palace at Phata Pursi

A.D. 1758 After defeating the Nawab of Bengal a year earlier at Plassey, for the first time, the British East India Company receives from the Mughal rulers the right to collect land taxes in Bengal.

A.D. 1857–8 The British crown imposes direct rule and the East India Company is dissolved.

A.D. 1870 Construction of the Red Sea telegraph brings a direct link with Britain.

farman (order) of Mughal emperor to East India Company

A.D. 1750   A.D. 1850   A.D. 1875

The First Indian Civilization

I N THE 1920s, archaeologists made an astonishing discovery. They found the remains of two great cities near the Indus River in northwestern India. The cities were called Mohenjo-Daro and Harappa. Before this, no one had known very much at all about India's earliest history, but it was now clear that there had been a vast urban civilization in the area as far back as 2600 B.C., and that it had lasted for almost a thousand years.

These ancient cities were very well organized. They had drainage systems, a network of roads, granaries, water tanks, and canals, and also raised citadels (fortresses) where the rulers lived. It is clear that the city dwellers traded with other civilizations, too, because Indus valley objects have been found as far away as Egypt and Mesopotamia. For some reason, this bustling culture went into a decline after 1700 B.C. It is possible that the climate became drier, causing crops to fail, or that the people destroyed their own environment, perhaps by overgrazing. No one is sure.

LOST CITY
Ruins of the citadel at Mohenjo-Daro. Like all the cities of the Indus Valley civilization, Mohenjo-Daro had a lower city and a high citadel. It was probably the largest of the Indus Valley cities. The raised stump at the back of the picture is the remains of a stupa—a monument containing relics of the Buddha. The stupa was erected long after the city declined.

TRADING TOKEN
Seals cast from soft soapstone may have been used as tokens for trading goods. This one shows a humped bull, or zebu. It comes from Mohenjo-Daro, and is over 4,000 years old. The symbols on the seal may have identified the traders.

MAKE A CLAY SEAL
You will need: rolling pin, modeling clay, board, ruler or measuring tape, blunt knife, scrap paper, pencil, modeling tool, white glue, paintbrush, white paint, string, plastic oven-drying modeling material.

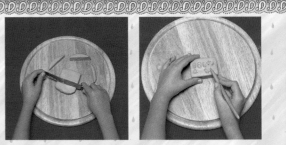

1 Use the rolling pin to roll out the modeling clay. When you have finished, you should have a rectangular slab of clay about 1 inch thick.

2 Carefully trim away the edges of the slab of clay so that they are neat and even. Your rectangle should now measure 4 x 3 inches.

3 Draw an animal shape onto the clay. (Practice drawing the shape on scrap paper first.) Carefully cut the pattern into the clay using a modeling tool.

CLAY WOMAN

A terra-cotta figurine from Mohenjo-Daro shows a woman in a headdress. The headdress looks as though it was made up of two baskets—a way of carrying heavy loads in India even today. The statue may have been a mother goddess or a doll or toy. Archaeologists have found groups of clay figurines like this that show people doing things around the house.

DESERTED VALLEY

Today, the Indus Valley is no longer a fertile place where people grow crops, but an arid (dry) landscape of bare soil. Around 1700 B.C., the cities of the Indus Valley were suddenly and rapidly depopulated. It is believed that a change in the course of the Indus River may have disturbed the primitive irrigation system, and led to a collapse in agriculture.

STORING FOOD

Large storage jars were used to keep and distribute food that was grown around Mohenjo-Daro. The fact that its people were able to store surplus food shows how settled and organized the society was.

INDUS VALLEY DANCER

This copper statuette shows a dancer from Mohenjo-Daro. The dancer has an elaborate hairstyle, necklaces, and lots of arm bangles. Thousands of years later, hairstyles and jewelry like this are still the ideal of what makes a woman look beautiful in India.

4 Roll out a 1-inch sausage-shaped piece of modeling clay. Bend it into a curved handle shape. Glue the handle to the slab.

5 Paint the clay slab with a single coat of white paint. This will give your seal a clean surface that will not stain or leave any dirty marks.

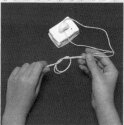

6 Loop the string through the handle of your seal. Knot the string to secure. Mold the plastic oven-drying modeling material into a slab shape.

7 Press the seal into the modeling material. Your pattern appears raised in reverse. Bake the material, following the instructions on the package.

The Noble People

A KING AND HIS PRIESTS
A raja (king) consults his Brahmin priests near a sacrificial fire. The relationship of the Brahmin and the raja became very close in the time of the Vedic hymns. Brahmins performed the sacrifice for the raja to bring him wealth, prosperity, and sons. When empires began to form after about 350 B.C., the Brahmins became the ministers of the king's government, because of their important role.

ABOUT 400 YEARS after the decline of the Indus Valley civilization, a new wave of people arrived in India from the northwest, probably from Central Asia. They were known as the Aryans, or "noble people." They lived in small groups or larger tribes. Gradually, they moved further into India and took over the part of the plains between the Indus and the Ganges rivers. At first, the Aryans lived by herding animals, but as they settled, they started growing crops instead.

The Aryans divided society into three castes (classes). These were made up of priests (Brahmin), warriors (Kshatriya), and property holders (Vaishya). There was a also a fourth caste of servants and laborers called Shudra, made up of the people that the Aryans had conquered. Each of the castes played a different role in an important Aryan custom—the offering of a burnt sacrifice of meat and grains to the gods in return for rains, wealth, and sons. The hymns of praise to the gods during this sacrifice were called the Vedas. They were composed in a language that was eventually called Sanskrit, meaning refinement. These Aryan customs and writings formed the basis of the Hindu religion.

OFFERING CUP

You will need: Plastic drinking cup, scissors, piece of medium card, white glue or tape, modeling clay, rolling pin, board, modeling tools, dark brown and reddish-brown paint, paintbrushes, kitchen towel, nontoxic varnish.

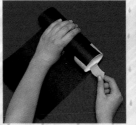

1 Cut off the top half of the plastic cup. Roll the piece of card into a tube shape. It should be wide enough for the bottom of the cup to sit into it neatly.

2 Overlap the edges of the rolled-up card. Glue or tape the edges to hold them in place. Fit the trimmed cup into the card tube, right side up.

3 Roll out the modeling clay. Cover the card tube with the clay. Use some of the clay to cover the plastic drinking cup, too. Leave the clay to dry.

PRIESTS

Brahmins wore a sacred white cotton cord across the chest. All boys of the Brahmin caste received the sacred cord at about the age of 11. It took nine years or more to learn a priest's duties. Brahmins were the only people allowed to teach the children of the three upper castes. People of these castes were called "twice-born," because they were accepted into adult life through a special ceremony. In one sacrificial hymn, the Brahmins come from the mouth of the higher being, or Cosmic Man.

WARRIORS

The warrior noble, or Kshatriya, was the next highest caste after the Brahmin. The raja, who was the protector of society, came from the Kshatriya class. It was his duty to safeguard the position of each caste, and to give money to the Brahmins. The Kshatriyas were thought to be the arms of the Cosmic Man.

ORDINARY PEOPLE

The Vaishyas were the common people of the Aryan clans. They were large in number and rich in wealth. They practiced agriculture and trade, and were thought to be the "thighs" of the Cosmic Man. They were above the peasants and people of no caste, who were considered "impure."

Offering cups were an important part of the ritual of the sacrifices that the Aryans made to the gods. The cups were always the same shape, and would have been filled with holy water.

4 Using a wooden modeling tool, carefully start to carve your chosen design into the modeling clay on the cup.

5 Finish carving the picture. Cut texture lines into the clay. This will help to make your finished cup look like it has been made from wood.

6 Paint the cup with dark brown paint. While it is still wet, wipe some of the paint off with kitchen towel, to give it a streaked look. Leave to dry.

7 Paint the cup with reddish-brown paint. The darker paint will still show through in places. Leave to dry. Give the cup two coats of varnish.

Buddhist India

THE CUSTOMS AND TEACHINGS of the Aryan people meant that the highest born Brahmins (priests) were the only ones who could be saved from life's suffering. People of other castes were not happy with this, and by 500 B.C. new religious practices began to develop. Siddharta Gautama was born into the warrior caste, but left his family at the age of 30 to seek spiritual enlightenment (freedom). He gained many followers during his lifetime and became known simply as the Buddha, which means enlightened. He taught what he called a "Middle Way" between pleasure and suffering, which everyone could follow regardless of their caste.

The Buddha's followers evolved into an order of monks called the sangha, who wandered from place to place with a begging bowl and survived on people's donations. Many important people, including kings and merchants, gave generously to the sangha and built monasteries for them to live in. After the Buddha's death, his followers honored him by building large domed monuments, called stupas.

From 272 B.C., King Ashoka encouraged the spread of Buddhism. Ashoka is said to have built an incredible 80,000 stupas, each with its own monastery.

RECORDED IN STONE
This relief from the A.D. 500s shows events from Buddha's life. Scenes, such as his departure from his father's palace and enlightenment under the bodhi tree, were recorded on monuments. There they could be read by many people.

GIFTS TO THE BUDDHA
The stupa at Sanchi was built by Ashoka and embellished by later monarchs. The dome is surrounded by a beautifully carved railing that shows scenes from the Buddha's life. At this stupa and several others at Sanchi, almost 900 short inscriptions have been found. Each one records the gifts of monks and ordinary people.

CAVE MONASTERY
In western India, cave monasteries were built among the rocks to house communities of monks. Buddhist monks needed to be alone so that they could meditate and follow the path to enlightenment.

ANCIENT AND MODERN
Modern monks in Sri Lanka worship an ancient statue of the Buddha. Buddhism was brought to Sri Lanka by Ashoka's son, Mahinda. The very oldest form of Buddhism, called Theravada, is still practiced in Sri Lanka today.

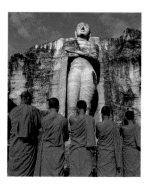

TIBETAN PRAYER HANGING
A painting of the Buddha on a prayer hanging in Tibet has a face that is more Central Asian than Indian. In Tibet, Buddhism grew into a new form called Vajrayana. This tradition often included secret teachings about rituals.

RELICS OF THE BUDDHA
A limestone carving at the great stupa in Nagarjunakonda, in eastern India, shows gods and men venerating (worshipping) the Buddha's relics. The relics are encased in the central mound of every stupa. Relics are pieces of bone or hair that Buddhists believe have come from the body of the Buddha.

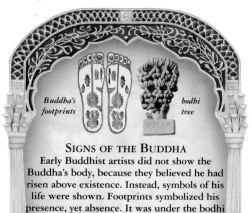

Buddha's footprints

bodhi tree

SIGNS OF THE BUDDHA
Early Buddhist artists did not show the Buddha's body, because they believed he had risen above existence. Instead, symbols of his life were shown. Footprints symbolized his presence, yet absence. It was under the bodhi tree that Buddha achieved enlightenment.

Hindu Gods and Goddesses

BUDDHISM REMAINED the dominant religion in India until about A.D. 200, but the religion of the Aryan people did not disappear. Instead, it evolved into new forms, which together became known as Hinduism. Many of the beliefs were the same, but Hinduism discouraged the Vedic practice of making animal sacrifices, and introduced new gods to replace the Aryan deities. Gradually, Hinduism took over from Buddhism, and has remained India's dominant religion ever since.

In the two main types of Hinduism—Vaishnavism and Shaivism—Hindus believe that one god (Vishnu or Shiva) rules the universe. From about A. D. 1000, some worshiped the goddess Devi instead. In each version, the Cosmic Man (the representation of the god on earth) takes on different forms depending on the task, so Hindu mythology seems to have hundreds of gods. In fact they are versions of Vishnu, Shiva, or Devi.

TERRIBLE GOD
Shiva appears in the form of a terrifying being wielding a trident. At times Shiva is associated with the destructive forces of the universe, and commands demonic beings, called ganas.

HAPPY GOD
The conch shell and the discus are the symbols of the god Vishnu, who is often shown with blue skin. Vishnu mainly brings happiness, preservation, and kingship. He stands on a lotus flower.

MAKE A GARLAND OF FLOWERS

You will need: Orange, yellow, red, pink, and white tissue paper, pencil, scissors, white glue, paintbrush, piece of string, darning needle.

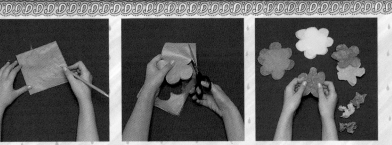

1 Draw simple flower shapes onto sheets of colored tissue paper. If you like, you can lay the sheets of paper in layers, one on top of the other.

2 Using scissors, cut out your flower shapes. Be careful not to tear the tissue paper. Cut the same number of flowers in each color.

3 Scrunch up the tissue flower shapes with your hands. Then uncrumple them, but don't smooth them out too much.

GANESHA

The elephant god, Ganesha, is the son of Shiva. He is god of wisdom and prosperity, and is known for his love of sweets. Ganesha is always illustrated traveling with a rat.

KRISHNA AND RADHA

The god Krishna was an incarnation of Vishnu on earth. Krishna was born as a cowherder. In his youth, he was supposedly adored by many women, but his favorite was Radha. The love of Radha and Krishna is the theme of many Hindu religious songs.

GODDESS OF DEATH AND WAR

Shiva's wife had many forms. The fiercest was Kali, the goddess of death. Here, she holds an array of weapons in her many arms. Kings often worshipped Kali before going into battle.

Hindus make garlands of fresh flowers to wear at festivals to honor their gods.

4 Glue the flower shapes together loosely in layers to make larger, single flowers. Use eight layers of tissue paper for each complete flower.

5 Now gently fluff up the layers of tissue paper with your fingers. This will make your flowers look much more realistic.

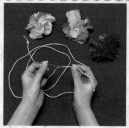

6 Measure a piece of string that is long enough to go around your neck. Start to thread the flowers onto the string to make a garland.

7 Thread all the tissue flowers onto the piece of string. When you have strung all of the flowers, tie a double knot in the string to complete it.

Epic Tales of the Gods

A DECISIVE BATTLE
Prince Arjuna and Krishna face the Kauravas on the battlefield. It is here that Krishna (painted blue) reveals that he is a god to Arjuna, and sings a song that tells him how to behave properly. Krishna's song is known as the *Bhagavad-Gita*.

BROTHERS IN ARMS
The five Pandava brothers are honored in this shrine. They are the heroes of the *Mahabharata* story. They struggle with the Kauravas to regain their kingdom, and are aided by Krishna. Each brother is known for a noble quality, such as heroism.

THE MOST IMPORTANT ancient stories of the Hindus are told in two great epics (long poems) called the *Ramayana* and the *Mahabharata*. No one is sure exactly who wrote them or when, but they were written down in their present form by A.D. 500. In both, the god Vishnu appears in different incarnations (forms) to save the earth from destruction, and to tell people about right and wrong.

In the *Ramayana*, Vishnu takes the form of the exiled prince Rama. His wife, Sita, is abducted by the demon Ravana and taken to a fortress in Lanka (present-day Sri Lanka). Rama rescues Sita with the help of the monkey god, Hanuman.

The *Mahabharata* is a much longer story, with many subplots. It tells of a bitter struggle between two families, the Pandavas and the Kauravas. Krishna, another human version of Vishnu, helps the Pandavas to defeat the Kauravas. Part of the *Mahabharata* is Krishna's advice on morality to the Pandava prince, Arjuna. It is called the *Bhagavad-Gita*, and it is given just before the last battle, which the Pandavas finally manage to win.

MAKE A RAMAYANA HEADDRESS
You will need: Ruler, pencil, 2 large sheets of thin red card, scissors, Scotch tape, strips of corrugated cardboard, red paint, paintbrushes, string, thumb tack, bright-colored paints, glue, tinfoil candy wrappers.

1 Use a ruler and pencil to draw two straight lines at an angle onto the card. Connect these lines with curved lines, as above. Cut out the shape.

2 Roll the card into a shape that is narrower at the top. The bottom of the card should be wide enough to fit your head. Seal the edges with tape.

3 Tape a strip of corrugated cardboard around the base of your headdress shape, but leave a gap at the back where the seam is.

RAMA ATTACKS THE DEMON ARMY

With the help of Hanuman and his army of monkeys, and an army of bears, Rama attacks the forces of the demon Ravana in Lanka. Rama is victorious in his battle and kills Ravana. He is then reunited with his wife, Sita.

MONKEY KING

Hanuman, leader of the monkeys of the forest, became Rama's most faithful follower. As Rama searched frantically for his wife, Sita, it was Hanuman who found her in Ravana's palace in Lanka. Hanuman led Rama and his monkey forces to Sita's rescue.

THE DOOMED KING

The demon king, Ravana, leads his demon generals. In the *Ramayana*, Ravana was the all-powerful king of the island of Lanka. However, a prophecy foretold that he would lose his life because of a woman. That woman turned out to be Sita.

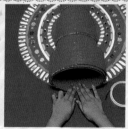

Hindus wear headdresses to act out scenes from the story of Rama and Sita.

4 Tape the cardboard strips around the middle and the top of your hat shape, again leaving a gap at the back. Paint the strips with red paint.

5 Measure the height of your headdress. Using a string tied to a thumb tack and a pencil, draw a circle with a diameter that matches the height of your headdress.

6 Carefully cut out the circle. Now use bright-colored paints and tinfoil candy wrappers to decorate your headdress in all the colors of the rainbow.

7 Leave the decorated circle to dry thoroughly. Then glue or tape it to the back of your headdress. Finally, decorate the headdress.

Houses of the Gods

A HINDU TEMPLE IS A LITTLE like a palace that has been built for a god to live in. In the old Aryan Vedic religion, people believed that the gods lived in the skies and were fed by the sacrificial fires. After each sacrifice, the altar was taken down. When Hinduism evolved, it adopted the Buddhist practice of building places of worship called stupas. Shaivas and Vaishnavas built beautiful temples, and invited their gods to come and live in them in the form of images, such as statues. Brahmin priests took care of the statues, and tended to their every need. The gods were woken, bathed, dressed, entertained, and fed each day. This practice of honoring a god's image is called puja, and is still central to Hinduism today.

By A.D. 500, temples were common. As kings converted to Hinduism, they built many huge temples across India, and lavished donations of money and tax revenue from farmlands upon them. By A.D. 1000, most Hindu temples were not only places of worship, but places where country people traded goods.

HONORING THE BUDDHA
This frieze is from a 2,000-year-old stupa at Amaravati, a Buddhist site in southern India. It shows men and gods honoring the feet of the Buddha. Puja (worship) was first practiced by Buddhists. It later became popular among Hindus, too.

TEMPLE TOWER
The temple to Shiva at Bhubaneshwar in Orissa was built in the A.D. 800s. The tower is the home of a linga, or symbol of Shiva. The tower itself is a mix of northern and southern Indian styles of temple. The central tower of another temple is present in the background of the picture. Kings often built several temples close to each other.

A SHRINE AT HOME
A man makes an offering at a shrine in his home. From early times, Hindus worshipped gods in the household, as well as in the temple. Most Hindus do not pray together—they pray alone, in private.

A PORTABLE SHRINE

This cloth was used as a portable shrine for worshipping the god Pabuji. Pabuji was a hero of the 1300s who was converted into a god. The pictures surrounding the figure of Pabuji represent scenes from his life, as they are told in a folk story. Folk priests in the northern state of Rajasthan went from village to village carrying cloths like these, to use as temples.

SYMBOL OF POWER

A gopuram (gate tower) at the Shiva temple at the city of Madurai, in Tamil Nadu. Gopurams were built by kings as symbols of power, each king trying to outdo his rivals. This gopuram is so huge, it is larger than the shrine inside the temple itself. Gopurams are covered in painted carvings and can be seen from afar.

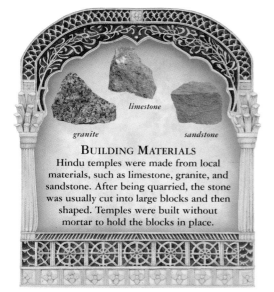

limestone

granite *sandstone*

BUILDING MATERIALS

Hindu temples were made from local materials, such as limestone, granite, and sandstone. After being quarried, the stone was usually cut into large blocks and then shaped. Temples were built without mortar to hold the blocks in place.

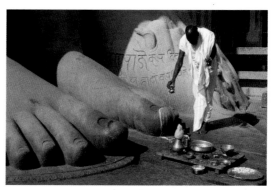

AT THE FEET OF THE SAINT

A worshipper performs puja (worship) to a saint in southern India. His image is so huge that the priests can only reach his toes to place flower and coconut offerings. When the image is bathed, scaffolding is erected to reach the head.

The Coming of Islam

THE MUSLIM RELIGION, called Islam—which means submission to God—was founded in Arabia (present-day Saudi Arabia) by a man named Mohammed in A.D. 622. It spread quickly into the countries around Arabia, but it took almost 400 years for Islam to reach India.

In A.D. 1007, Sultan Mahmud, the Muslim leader of the city of Ghazni in Afghanistan, started a series of attacks on northern India to loot the rich temples there. More Islamic leaders followed his example, and by A.D. 1206, Muslim Turks from Central Asia had founded a new kingdom, or Sultanate, based in the city of Delhi. The Delhi Sultanate ruled the region for 300 years.

Islam gradually spread among ordinary people. Islamic sufis (mystics) played an important role in spreading the message of God's love for all people. They worshipped in a very emotional style at their countryside shrines, in a way that the Hindu peasants could understand. By the 1700s, almost a quarter of India's population was Muslim. They showed great tolerance toward other religions and cultures, especially toward the Hindu faith.

BEAUTIFUL WRITING
This page is from a Persian commentary on the holy book of Muslims, the *Quran*. Muslims were not allowed to represent images, such as humans, animals, or flowers, in art. Instead they developed calligraphy (the art of beautiful writing).

SEAFARING SETTLERS
The Indian Ocean was controlled by Muslim traders from about A.D. 700. They arrived along the southwestern coast of India on their way to Indonesia and China, and were among the earliest Muslims to settle in India. These traders followed Muslim law. Different Muslim laws spread in India through further Muslim invasions from Turkey and Afghanistan in the 1100s and 1200s.

FROM TEMPLE TO MOSQUE
The Quwat al-Islam, a large mosque in Delhi, was built out of parts of destroyed temples of older faiths. It has two architectural features that were introduced to India by Islam. One feature is the arch, the other is the use of mortar for cementing bricks together. The mosque was built by the Delhi Sultanate in 1193.

HOLY MEN
Sufis (mystics) gather together to pray. Sufism was a type of Islam that preached that people's souls can communicate to God through ecstatic music, singing, and dancing. Sufism came into prominence in Persia in the A.D. 900s. By about 1100, it had also gained a foothold in the northwest of India.

FAMILY TOMB
A man bicycles toward a tomb of one of the later Sultans of Delhi. The tomb is in the gardens of the Lodi family, the last rulers of the Delhi Sultanate. The last Lodi Sultan was defeated in battle by the Mughal prince Babur, in

SUFI SHRINE
This tomb-shrine, or dargah, in Rajgir, honors a famous sufi saint. Sufi teachers were called pirs, or shaikhs. They often had a large number of followers.

The Sikh Society

AS ISLAM SPREAD through northern India, Hinduism and Islam existed side by side. In the Punjab region of northern India, a new religion emerged that had elements of both. It was called Sikhism, and was founded by a man called Guru (teacher) Nanak (1469–1539). Sikhism rejected the strict Hindu caste system and adopted the Islamic idea that all people are equal before God, but it kept many aspects of Hindu ritual. Sikhs worshipped in temples called gurdwaras (abode of the gurus). After Nanak, there were nine more gurus. The fifth, Arjan, founded the Golden Temple at Amritsar, which later became the holiest of all gurdwaras. He also wrote the Sikh holy book, or *Adi Granth*.

In the 1600s, the Muslim Mughal rulers in Delhi became concerned about the growth of this new religion. They began to persecute the Sikhs, and killed Arjan and another guru. The tenth guru, Gobind Singh, decided that Sikhs should protect themselves, and founded a military order called the khalsa. Members carried a comb and dagger, wore a steel bangle and breeches, and did not cut their hair. Sikh men took the title Singh (lion). After Gobind Singh's death in 1708, there were no more gurus, but Sikhs continued to live by the teachings of the *Adi Granth*.

LETHAL TURBAN
A Sikh war turban is decorated with weapons that could be removed and used against the enemy during battle. Metal throwing rings could slice heads off, and "claws" were for disembowelling people.

THE GOLDEN TEMPLE
The greatest Sikh temple is the Golden Temple in the Sikh holy city of Amritsar. The temple was built by Guru Arjan Singh (1581-1606). Its white marble walls and domes are decorated with gold. The city of Amritsar is named after the lake that surrounds the temple. Sikhs worship in their temples in large congregations (groups). Free kitchens are attached to Sikh temples, where all can eat.

SYMBOLIC COMB
This close-up picture of a Sikh turban shows the kangha, a comb that is pinned to the center. The kangha is one of the five signs of the Sikh religion. Sikh men do not cut their hair—another sign of Sikhism.

THE SACRED BOOK
The *Adi Granth* is the sacred book of the Sikhs. Its text was compiled by Guru Arjan Singh in the late 1500s. After the death of the last teacher, Guru Gobind Singh, Sikhs came to accept these scriptures as the symbol of God. They took over the role of the teacher from the Gurus.

A MILITARY MAHARAJA
The Maharaja Ranjit Singh (1799–1838) holds court. The water tank of the Golden Temple can be seen in the background. Ranjit Singh led the Sikh army to victory against Afghan warlords and the collapsing Mughal Empire. He established a separate Sikh kingdom in the Punjab region of India.

AN ABLE WARRIOR
A Sikh soldier sits on a cushion in this portrait from the 1800s. When the British ruled India, they recruited many Sikhs into their army. Sikhs were regarded as one of India's most warlike peoples.

The Mughal Empire

I**N 1526, A PRINCE** from the area now called Uzbekistan invaded India from the northwest. His name was Babur. He swept across the country with a powerful army and soon arrived in Delhi, where he defeated the Sultanate and founded a new empire. His successors were eventually called the Mughals. The Mughal Empire was the last important dynasty of India before the British arrived in the 1700s.

Babur's grandson, Akbar, who ruled from 1556 to 1605, was a great Mughal leader. Although he was Muslim, he was tolerant of other religions, and took Hindu princesses as his wives. Forty years later, the warlike Mughal ruler Aurangzeb returned to a stricter form of Islam and expanded the empire. The Mughals were patrons of the arts, and built glorious

palaces, gardens, and tombs. Many of India's most precious works of art date from this era. Persian was the language of their court, but they also spoke Urdu, a mixture of Persian, Arabic, and Hindi.

ORDERLY COURTIERS
Mughal nobles had to take part in court rituals. They had to arrive punctually at court, and line up in rows. Their dress and posture were very important. The cummerbund tied around the waist and the turban were signs of self-control. Courtiers guarded the palace, taking turns.

THE FIRST MUGHAL EMPEROR
Babur defeats Ibrahim Lodi, the last sultan of Delhi, at the Battle of Panipat in 1526. Babur invaded India because he was unable to recapture his own homeland in Samarkand.

MAKE A LACQUERED STORAGE BOX
You will need: Pencil, ruler, sheets of card, scissors, Scotch tape, newspaper, wallpaper paste or flour and water, bowl, fine sandpaper, paint in white and bright colors, paintbrushes, nontoxic varnish.

1 Scale the shape above to the size you want your box to be, and copy the shape onto the card. Cut out the shape, and stick the edges with Scotch tape to form a box.

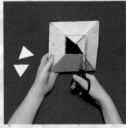

2 Draw four card triangles with sides the same length as the top of the box. Tape the triangles together to make a pyramid. Cut off the top.

3 Add newspaper strips to the paste, or flour and water, to make papier mâché. Cover the box and lid with three layers of papier mâché. Dry between layers.

A POEM IN STONE

The emperor Shah Jahan commemorated his wife Mumtaz Mahal (who died in childbirth) by building this magnificent mausoleum. It was built between 1631 and 1648, and was later named the Taj Mahal. It is built of white marble from Rajasthan. The Taj Mahal is one of the most magnificent buildings in the world, and it is the high point of Mughal art.

JADE HOOKAH

This Mughal period hookah (pipe) is made from precious green jade. During Mughal times, the culture of the court reached a high point in Indian history, and many fine pieces like this were made.

RED PALACE

The Red Fort in Agra is one of the palaces built by Akbar. The Mughal emperors broke with the tradition of kings living in tents, and built sumptuous residences in their capital cities.

Lacquered boxes were popular with women of the royal court for storing jewelery.

4 When the papier mâché is dry, sand any rough edges with sandpaper. Add squares of cardboard for feet. Paint the box and the lid white.

5 Allow the painted box and lid to dry. Draw a pattern onto the box and lid. You could copy the pattern shown above, or use your own design.

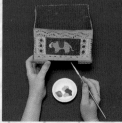

6 Paint the lid and the box, including the feet, with the bright-colored paints. Use the pattern that you have drawn as a guide. Leave to dry.

7 To complete, paint the box and lid with a coat of nontoxic varnish. Leave to dry thoroughly, then add a final coat of varnish. Your box is now finished.

The Symbols of Royalty

OVER THE CENTURIES, kings of many different religions ruled India. The titles that they took and the objects that surrounded them often had symbolic significance, and they tell us a lot about their role as leaders. From the time of Ashoka, around 250 B.C., the ruler of the empire was called a cakravartin (wheel-turner). The wheel was a Buddhist symbol for the world, so this suggested that the king made the world go around. Objects that were symbols of royalty included sceptres, crowns, and yak-tail fly whisks. The most important object was the chatra (umbrella), which signified the king's protection of his realm.

Later, Hindu kings (called maharajadhirajas) developed the idea that the god Vishnu lived within them. When Islam arrived, the sultans showed their obedience to the caliph, the head of Islam in Baghdad, by taking titles such as nasir (helper). Mughals took Persian titles such as padshah, which simply means emperor.

DISPLAY OF POWER
A Mughal emperor rides through the city on top of an elephant, a symbol of royalty. Kings often processed through their cities to display their power and majesty. They were always followed by attendants and courtiers.

THE MARKS OF A KING
A picture of the man/god Rama's foot depicts the lotus, conch shell, umbrella, fly whisk, and other royal symbols. People thought that a world-ruling king was born with special features. Among these were unique marks on the soles of his feet and the palms of his hands, which foretold that he would be emperor.

MAKE A CHAURI

You will need: Strip of corrugated cardboard that measures 1 x 10 inches, raffia, scissors, Scotch tape, white glue, 8-inch piece of dowel, modeling clay, gold paint and a contrasting color, paintbrushes, tinfoil candy wrappers.

1 Put the strip of card on a covered, flat surface. Cut strips of raffia. Carefully tape the strands of raffia to the card. Leave your chauri to dry.

2 Wrap the card and raffia around the dowel, and glue it in place. Keep the card ¾ inch from the top, so that the dowel supports the raffia.

3 Tape the card and raffia band tightly in place to make sure that it will not come undone when you use your whisk. Leave the whisk to dry.

A KING'S HALO

The king in this procession has a halo surrounding his head. From Mughal times, it was believed that rulers were blessed with the divine light of wisdom. This was represented in pictures by a halo.

ROYAL CUSHION

Raja Ram Singh of Jodhpur sits with his nobles. Only the king may sit on a cushion. The Rajputs were the kings of northern India, who fought against Muslim invaders, but later became their most important military allies under the Mughals.

ROYAL RAMA

Rama, the human form of the god Vishnu, sits with his wife Sita and his brothers. He holds a bow, a symbol of courage. Also seen are other symbols of royalty—an umbrella and a yak-tail whisk.

The fly whisk was a symbol of a Hindu king's power.

4 Make lots of small beads from the modeling clay. Glue these onto the dowel in a circle, about 1 inch below the strip of card. Leave to dry.

5 Paint the dowel and beads with two coats of gold paint. Leave it to dry. Then paint a pattern on the strip of card and the dowel, in different colors.

6 When the paint is dry, glue pieces of colored tinfoil to your chauri. The more decorations you add, the more it will look like a real chauri.

Entertainment

THE ROYAL COURTS OF Mughal India were places of marvelous entertainment. Courtiers listened to poetry and music every day. They loved riddles and word games, and in contests, poets were given half of a verse and asked to finish it. Different art forms were connected to each other. For example, the *Natyashastra*, an ancient text about dance and drama, includes a long section on music. Dancers were also storytellers, using hand gestures to show meaning.

Northern and southern India developed their own musical traditions—Hindustani in the north and Karnatak in the south. Islam introduced new instruments, such as the sitar (a stringed instrument) and the tabla (a drum). Outside the courts, religion played a part in the development of singing. Muslim mystics sang and played musical pieces called qawwali, and Hindus sang songs to Krishna.

JOYFUL OCCASION
Drummers and trumpeters at the Mughal court joyfully proclaim the birth of Akbar's son, Prince Salim. Music was often used to announce celebrations. Though they enjoyed royal patronage and were often renowned for their talent, musicians, dancers, and actors were generally considered to be of low social standing.

INSTRUMENTAL BIRD
An instrument called a sarangi has been finely carved in the shape of a peacock. The sarangi was played with a bow, and usually accompanied the dance performances of courtesans during late Mughal times.

MAKE A PAIR OF ANKLETS
You will need: Measuring tape, garden wire, pliers, strips of red felt, scissors, glue or Scotch tape, darning needle, strong thread, silver bells.

1 Measure the diameter of your ankle. Multiply this number by three, then add 1 ½ inches for a loop. Use the pliers to cut two pieces of wire to this length.

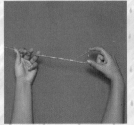

2 Loop the first cut piece of wire around itself about three times. Twist it tightly as you go. Then twist the second piece of wire in the same way.

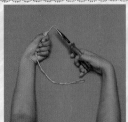

3 Using the pliers, bend one end of each strip of twisted wire to form a loop. Bend the other end to form a hook. These make a fastener.

FOLK DANCING

A decorative border shows figures linking hands in a Punjabi folk dance. Ordinary village people danced to celebrate births, weddings, and many other special occasions. Each dance usually involved lots of dancers.

ON A STRING

A woman from Rajasthan plays with a yo-yo. Games with balls and strings were not expensive, so they could be enjoyed by both rich and poor people. Many other kinds of games were afforded only by the wealthy.

ENTERTAINING AT COURT

Dancers perform the style of dance called a Kathak for the great Mughal emperor, Akbar. Dance was a popular form of entertainment at court. Many of the complicated dance styles popular in India today originated at the courts of kings in ancient times. The dances performed at court often told a story.

Anklets were worn by dancers who performed at ceremonies in the royal courts of the Mughals.

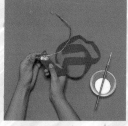

4 Cut out two strips of felt that are slightly longer than your strips of wire. Glue or tape a felt strip onto the end of the twisted wire.

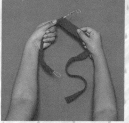

5 Wrap the felt around the wire, overlapping the edges of the felt. Glue the end of the felt to the place where you began. Wrap the second wire strip.

6 Thread a darning needle with a piece of thread. Sew lots of tiny silver bells to the felt that is covering your wire loops.

7 Repeat your stitches several times to make sure that the bells stay firmly in place. Add more bells, so that you cover both anklets completely.

Games and Sports

MANY GAMES DEVELOPED in the royal courts, where people had leisure time on their hands. One of these games, called caturanga, developed into the modern game of chess. Caturanga referred to the four parts of the army—the infantry, chariots, cavalry, and elephants. It had different rules from modern chess, though it is not known exactly what these rules were. The game was played with dice, and up to four players may have taken part at once.

Outdoor sports were usually associated with shikar (hunting), and included archery, falconry (hunting with birds of prey), and horsemanship. Muslim rulers brought the game of polo, which was played on horseback, from Persia.

Religious fairs and festivals gave ordinary people the chance to play games, too. Cockfighting, ramfighting, and wrestling were important. Springtime was the season of playfulness. The ancient springtime festival of Holi is associated with love and play, and people had great fun throwing colored powders and water over each other. Social roles were relaxed during the games of Holi, and people from different castes mixed freely. Holi is still celebrated today.

IMPORTANT PIECES
Sandstone and terra-cotta dice and other game pieces were discovered in the Indus valley. We cannot be sure which games these dice were used for. However, later Indian literature has recorded the importance of dice in playing games.

BOARD GAME
Archaeologists have found board games, such as the one pictured above, and toy animals in the Indus valley. These show that the Indus people must have enjoyed playing with toys and games.

A DANGEROUS SPORT
Wrestling was a favorite sport as long ago as 1000 B.C., and many kings had the title malla (wrestler). Wrestlers endured strict diets and physical training in camps called akharas. Wrestling could be a highly dangerous activity. One inscription tells of a wrestler who was accidentally killed during a match.

DEER HUNTER

A Mughal king hunts deer. Hunting was an important activity. Like active battle, it was an occasion to display the manhood of the king. The preferred prey were lions, tigers, boars, and deer. In Mughal times, the emperor would hold secret meetings, and put his closest servants to the test during the hunt.

PLAYING AT WARFARE

Mughal nobles play a game of polo. Polo was first played in Persia, and was introduced to India by Muslim conquerors in the 1200s. The game was originally intended to train cavalry (soldiers on horseback), since it developed good horse-handling skills and taught riders how to maneuvre at close quarters. Under the Mughals, polo became a popular sport among the nobility. However, it has never lost its military associations, and the Indian army still has a polo team to this day.

FLYING A KITE

A Mughal woman flies a kite. Kite-flying was a favorite sport in Mughal times. Competitions were so fierce that kite-fliers would dip the strings of their kites in crushed glass to cut down their rivals' kites from the sky.

A GAME OF STRATEGY

A Mughal period chess set made from painted ivory. Chess was used to educate princes, ministers, and nobles at court, and to sharpen their planning skills. The most important chess board piece—the king—has the least power, since he acts through those around him. This was similar to how Indians viewed their own king.

The Importance of Animals

ANIMALS WERE A PART OF everyday life throughout Indian history. Cows, oxen, water buffaloes, camels, horses, and elephants carried loads, were used for transportation and helped with farming. Hindus began to see the cow as the source of all life, and the most important animal of all. It became protected and holy, and to this day, Hindus are forbidden to harm them.

People kept pets, too, especially birds. They had peacocks in their gardens, and caged parrots, which were often taught how to speak. Muslim nobles also kept pigeons.

Animals played an important part in Hindu myths. For example, the god Vishnu incarnated himself as a turtle and a boar to save the world. Shiva's son Ganesha had an elephant's head, and the man/god Rama's most faithful companion was Hanuman, king of the forest monkeys. In the *Pancatantra* fables, each animal symbolized a human virtue or vice. Lions, tigers, and elephants were considered powerful, noble, brave, and proud, but dogs were viewed as unclean creatures with no self-respect. Jackals and herons were greedy and cunning, and monkeys were playful and foolish.

SYMBOL OF ROYALTY

Lions became the most common symbol of courage and nobility in India. They feature on this Ashokan pillar from around 250 B.C. This pillar was adopted as the symbol of the Indian republic in 1948.

MYTHICAL MAKARA

The makara is one of the mythical animals of India. It was a cross between an alligator and a tortoise. Makaras were a favorite animal with artists, and they often appear as decorations on stupas and temples.

MIGHTY ELEPHANTS

Elephants were viewed as strong and supporting, no doubt because they were often used to carry heavy loads. It was believed that at the end of the earth, heavenly elephants held up the sky. Elephants were also believed to be fierce and violent, and they were favored for use in battle. The best elephants were from Orissa, in eastern India, and from Sri Lanka.

CHARMING THE SNAKES

A snake charmer coaxes a cobra from a basket to amuse the Hindu god, Shiva. Snake charmers were known for their ability to lure and mesmerize snakes. They did this, not through the noise of their flute, but by using the movement of their hands and body to hold the reptile's attention. Snake charmers are still popular

CAT AND MOUSE

A cat sits inside a palace, while a mouse escapes across the roof. Cats were not usually treated as pets, but were tolerated as part of the household because they played an important role in controlling vermin, such as rats.

parrot

TALKATIVE PARROTS

Parrots and other talking birds were kept by wealthy people in cities in India. The birds were trained to speak by the people of the court. Since medieval times, many stories tell of parrots who blurted out the secrets of the palace in front of visitors!

BEAUTIFUL GUARDIANS

Peacocks were kept in gardens to help ward off snakes and to add to the beauty of the surroundings. They were also exported to the courts of emperors in Rome, China, and Persia as exotic gifts. The peacock's brilliant plumage inspired the design of many textile patterns in India.

Writing and Language

A WOODEN INSCRIPTION
This wooden tablet contains a Buddhist text written in a script called Kharosthi. It was the script of a group of people who lived in northwestern India from the first to the third centuries A.D. The kings who ruled them wanted their people to follow Buddhism.

THE EARLIEST KNOWN WRITING IN INDIA has been found on some seals from the ancient civilization of the Indus valley, but no one has yet been able to figure out what the symbols mean. Later, when the Aryan people arrived, they brought a language with them that then developed into a number of different regional languages. There was one formal version of all these, which was called Sanskrit.

In about 300 B.C., a new form of script (writing) appeared, called Brahmi. The Buddhist king Ashoka used this script to inscribe proclamations on rocks and pillars all over his empire, and by about 100 B.C., Brahmi was used throughout India.

Early Indian documents were written on sheaves of palm leaf or bark, which were then threaded together. Important documents that needed to last for a long time were engraved on copper plates. The coming of Islam brought the Persian language to India, along with Arabic writing, which was developed into an art form called calligraphy. By Mughal times, paper and ink were replacing older methods of record keeping.

CARVED IN STONE
A stone inscription from A.D. 900 on the pedestal of a Buddhist image from eastern India is written in Sanskrit. The image was given by a Buddhist monk for the benefit of his parents and teacher. The inscription is in an eastern form of nagari, the script used for modern Hindi.

MAKE A SUTRA

You will need: Two pieces of balsa wood or thick card 12 x 3 ½ inches, dark brown paint, paintbrushes, clear nontoxic varnish, large sheet of white paper, cold tea, scissors, ruler, pencil or bradawl, large darning needle, string or twine.

1 Brush the two 12 x 3 ½-inch rectangular pieces of balsa wood or card with brown paint, so that they look like dark wood. Leave to dry.

2 Varnish your painted book covers. Leave them to dry. Give them a second coat, then a third. The extra coats will give the book a laquered finish.

3 Crumple the sheet of paper so that it wrinkles. Uncrumple it, lay it flat, and paint it with cold tea. Leave it to dry. This makes it look old.

MUGHAL PAINTER AND SCRIBE

A young painter from the Mughal court, named Manohar, sits with the scribe Mohammad Husain al-Kashmiri surrounded by an inkwell, a pen box, books, and letters. They are writing in Persian, the language of the Mughal court and administration.

A MUGHAL WRITING SET

A jewel-inlaid box that dates back to Mughal times contains writing materials. These include a letter opener, a pen, a spoon, and a built-in inkwell.

INSCRIBED TOWER

An extract from the *Quran*, the Muslim holy book, decorates the Qutb Minar, a 235-foot-high tower in Delhi. The tower was built in the A.D. 1200s by Qutb-ud-Din Aibak, the first Muslim sultan of Dehli, to celebrate his victory over the Hindu kings. The art of beautiful writing, or calligraphy, was highly developed in Islamic cultures.

Sutras were religious texts. They were written like a code and needed a commentary to explain them.

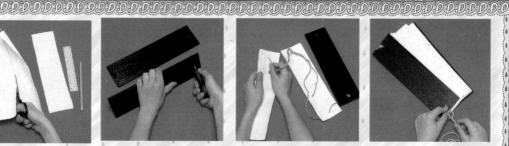

4 When it is completely dry, cut the crumpled paper into rectangular pieces that measure 11 ½ x 3 inches. These will be the pages of your book.

5 Mark a point in the middle of each book cover, about ¾ inch from each short edge. Use a pencil or bradawl to make holes in the book covers.

6 Put the paper pages between the two book covers. Use a large needle to thread string or twine through the paper and the book covers.

7 Knot the ends of the string or twine tightly. Make sure that the knot is bigger than the hole in the book cover, so that the pages stay in place.

Homes of Rich and Poor

Houses in India differed according to social class. Poor people made their homes out of mud, clay, and thatch. Materials such as these do not last long, so few of these houses' have survived. By about 600 B.C., wealthier people were building houses made of brick and stone. It is thought that people's caste determined not only the part of a town or city that they lived in, but also what color they painted their homes. The Brahmins of Jodhpur in Rajasthan, for example, painted their houses blue.

A wealthy man's house from about A.D. 400 had a courtyard and an outer room where guests were entertained. Behind this were the inner rooms, where the women of the house stayed and where food was cooked. Beyond the house itself, there were often gardens and fountains surrounded by an outside wall. Homes like this stayed much the same in design over many centuries.

Royal palaces were more elaborate. They had many courtyards and enclosures surrounded by numerous walls. These were to protect the king from beggars and servants who might make a nuisance of themselves. Unlike ordinary homes, palaces changed in design with each new wave of rulers.

DECORATED DOORSTEP
Pictures in chalk and rice powder were drawn on the doorsteps of houses. In time, they came to signify prosperity and good luck. Making such drawings was one of 64 forms of art that a cultured person was expected to be able to do.

birdcage

mango leaves hung for good luck

water trough

courtyard

MOUNTAIN HOMES
These modern mountain homes made from mud and thatch continue a tradition that is thousands of years old. Unlike valley homes, they have to be well insulated for protection against the colder climate.

THE GOOD LIFE
Life in a rich man's household was divided between the inner area, where he slept and ate, and the outer regions, dominated by a courtyard where he entertained friends, read, listened to music, and strolled in the garden. Here, salons (groups) of men would meet to discuss life and politics.

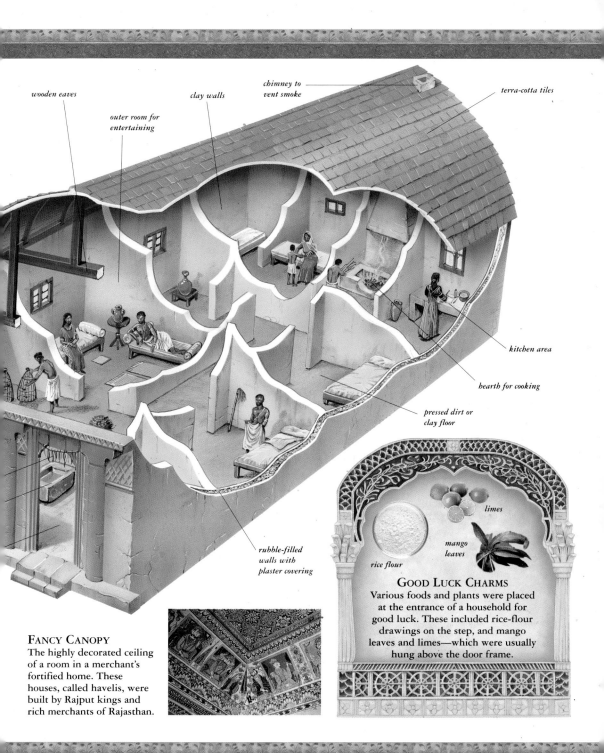

wooden eaves

outer room for entertaining

clay walls

chimney to vent smoke

terra-cotta tiles

kitchen area

hearth for cooking

pressed dirt or clay floor

rubble-filled walls with plaster covering

FANCY CANOPY
The highly decorated ceiling of a room in a merchant's fortified home. These houses, called havelis, were built by Rajput kings and rich merchants of Rajasthan.

limes

mango leaves

rice flour

GOOD LUCK CHARMS
Various foods and plants were placed at the entrance of a household for good luck. These included rice-flour drawings on the step, and mango leaves and limes—which were usually hung above the door frame.

A Woman's Place

ORDINARY WOMEN did not have an easy life in India. They toiled in the fields and threshed the wheat. In some parts of India, and among Muslims, women had to dress very modestly, and some were not allowed to go out at all. Women from rich families were symbols of a man's wealth. The more wives he had, the better, since it showed that he was rich enough to take care of them. Kings had several wives, too, because marrying women from different regions was a way of forming alliances. Very rarely, queens became leaders. Queen Raziya, for example, was sultan in the 1200s.

For almost 2,000 years in Indian art and literature, women ideally have had long hair, almond-shaped eyes, a sweet bird-like voice, and a shy manner. Sometimes they were portrayed as romantic heroines, such as Rama's virtuous wife, Sita, in the *Ramayana*. Hinduism also had many goddesses. Saraswati was the goddess of learning, Lakshmi was the the goddess of wealth, and Durga was the goddess of warfare.

IDEAL BEAUTY
This woman has large, almond-shaped eyes—the ideal of beauty in ancient India. Women lined their eyes with a black paste called collyrium, to accentuate the almond shape.

QUEST FOR KNOWLEDGE
Female Hindu ascetics (who practice self-denial) surround their leader in a holy hermitage. Rarely could women abandon a worldly life for spiritual pursuits, as men did. Usually, only widows were allowed to take the spiritual path.

TIE A SARI
You will need: Silky or cotton fabric 4 ½ yards x 40 inches, large safety pin. To make a decorated border for your sari, dip a cork into gold paint and print a pattern along one long edge of the fabric. Leave to dry.

1 Hold one corner of the fabric to your stomach, with the decorated border on the outside. Wrap the long side of the fabric once around your waist.

2 Make a number of pleats where the fabric comes back to the front again. Make them as even as you can. The pleats act as the sari's underskirt.

3 Tuck the pleated section into the waist of the underskirt. You could hold the pleats in place with safety pins while you practice tying the sari.

MORE THAN ONE WIFE

The Mughal emperor, Shah Jahan, is shown with one of his wives, Qudsia Begum. Both Hindu and Muslim men of rank often took more than one wife. Though this increased the chance of producing heirs, it could also create jealousy within the royal household.

COVERED HAIR

These women from Rajasthan cover their hair with their saris. The spread of Islam influenced the habits of Hindu women in northern India. They had to dress according to what was considered modest by Muslims.

HARD DAY'S WORK

Female laborers pick tea in northeastern India. Though tea was not drunk in India, women worked in the fields to cultivate other crops. Low-caste peasant women made up the most exploited class in society.

A sari is a single large cloth that covers both the upper and lower body. Saris were first worn in eastern India over a 1,000 years ago.

FOOD FOR THE FAMILY

A woman prepares food for her family. Women of the laboring classes have had a hard life throughout India's history. They not only worked in the fields, but were responsible for the household work, too.

4 Take the excess length of fabric in your left hand, and feed it all the way around your back. Be careful so that the pleats don't come out.

5 Now take the rest of the fabric in your right hand and lift it up so that it is level with your shoulders. Do this in front of a mirror, if you can.

6 Swing the fabric over your left shoulder. The fabric should fall in gentle folds from your shoulder, across your body, to your waist.

7 Carefully pin the fabric to the shoulder of your T-shirt, to keep it in place. Look in a mirror to see if the sari fits well. If it doesn't, try again!

Village India

A VILLAGE HOME
Cane houses with thatched roofs have been typical in the villages of eastern India for hundreds of years. The stone foundation raises the floor of this house above light flooding levels. Other building materials for village structures include mud, clay, and wood.

THROUGHOUT HISTORY, most people in India have lived in the country instead of in towns, so village life has always been an essential part of Indian civilization. This worked in one of two ways. Some villages were tribal, which meant that the villagers organized their own lives and were independent from other rulers. In other villages, the people were peasants, which meant that they were controlled by local rulers or emperors, and had to pay taxes.

From medieval times onward, more and more villagers became peasants. Whether they were peasants or tribal, however, people had plenty of contact with towns and cities, because they provided city-dwellers with food. The taxes demanded by rulers often took the form of food, too.

Villagers farmed in different ways, depending upon where they lived. In drier and higher regions, it was difficult to grow crops. Villagers in these areas grew a few crops and kept animals. They often remained tribal. In the fertile plains and river basins, rice cultivation supported densely populated and complex societies, which grew into great empires.

A CRUCIAL CROP
Terraced paddy fields in the hills of eastern India have been flooded with water. Rice cultivation requires elaborate irrigation techniques, since the plant's root must be submerged in water. Rice cultivation was the dominant agricultural activity in central, eastern, and southern India in the past, the same as now. Rice was a high-yield crop, and it could feed large masses of people. This made it possible for advanced societies and huge empires to grow.

BULLOCK CART
A villager and his bullock arrive at the construction site of a Mughal palace. Bullock carts were the most common vehicles in villages. They carried heavy loads of grain and rice, and building materials, too.

WASHING CLOTHES
Village dhobi (washermen) clean clothes in a river. They scrub the clothes on stone slabs next to the river. Behind the dhobi, men are working on a building site.

THE MARKET
A Mughal period painting shows food being sold at a village market. A cow is being milked, and rice and water are being sold. Each village or cluster of villages had a street market where produce was bought and sold.

barley

lentils

basmati rice

STAPLE FOODS
Rice, barley, and lentils were the most common foods grown in rural villages. Dishes that used these ingredients formed the people's main diet. Since the village poor generally could not afford meat, lentils were an important source of protein.

TYPICAL VILLAGE LIFE
A caravan (a group of merchants traveling together) passes by along a river near Murshidabad with three villages nearby. Villagers bathe by the river and plough the fields. Horses and camels can be seen in a horse market. In the foreground, an ascetic receives visitors.

Money and Trade

TRADE WITH DISTANT COUNTRIES has been important for India as far back as the ancient civilization of the Indus Valley. Later, trade routes became established up and down the length of India, and also with faraway places. Luxurious and precious goods, such as spices, jewels, ebony, ivory, and teak, were the main trade objects. One highly prized import was silk from China.

The first coins in India, which had very simple designs, date from about 500 B.C. They were probably introduced from Persia (modern Iran). By about 100 B.C., coins were used to pay for goods and services in city markets and courts, but they were less common in villages, where people simply exchanged goods, a practice called bartering. Bartering remained the normal way of trading for villagers until Mughal times.

Many different types of coins were produced, including square ones. Some had portraits of kings and gods on them, and these were often inscribed with the name of the ruling king. They were made of gold, silver, copper, and alloys (mixes of metals). Silver was often used for the best coins, but supplies sometimes ran out when silver was in demand for making statues and ornaments instead.

HEADS OR TAILS

A king of the Gupta dynasty with a stringed instrument is stamped on a gold coin that dates from around A.D. 350. Portraits of ancient Hindu royalty were often to be found on coins. Few other likenesses, such as sculptures or carvings, exist of ancient Hindu kings.

SHELLING OUT

Cowrie shells were used as currency (money) in coastal areas. They were also used inland when precious metals were scarce. Cowries were the lowest form of coinage. In one court poem, it is said that King Ramapala of Bengal paid his army in cowrie shells.

TRADE ROAD FOR SILK

The Silk Road stretched for around 4,500 miles from China to Anatolia (modern Turkey) and beyond. It was a trade route for items such as silk, jewels, and spices. Travelers along the Silk Road also brought new ideas. China and Central Asia were introduced to Buddhism, and many Chinese pilgrims came to India via the Silk Road.

saffron

TRADING IN SPICE
Saffron is an aromatic spice grown in northern India. Sandalwood is a musky-smelling wood, produced mainly in the south. Both were rare and valuable, and were among India's most prized trading items. They were exported to the Middle East and to China.

ARAB TRADING VESSEL
This painting shows an Arab trading ship. The Indian Ocean became an important trading zone after the rise of Islam in the A.D. 600s. The ocean linked the powerful empires of Arabia to eastern lands, such as India, Southeast Asia, and China. Muslim merchants ruled the seas from c. A.D. 700 until the coming of the Europeans in the 1500s.

TRADERS TRAVELING TOGETHER
A wall mural from Rajasthan shows a caravan (a group of merchants traveling together). Camels were ideal for travel in western Rajasthan, which is mostly desert. From Mughal times, Rajasthani merchants were famous throughout India for being good at making money.

COIN MEDALLION
A gold coin of the Mughal emperor Jahangir (1605-1627) has a portrait on one side and a Persian inscription on the other. This coin was probably not used in trade, but instead was worn as a sign of the emperor's favor. Using coins as decorations—especially if the coins were made of gold—dates back to the A.D. 100s. At that time, Roman coins were made into jewelery in southern India.

Dress and Accessories

Clothing has always been very simple in India. Noble people, both men and women, usually wore a single piece of fabric that was draped around the hips, drawn up between the legs, then fastened securely again at the waist. Women wore bodices above the waist, but men were often bare-chested. Although their clothes were simple, people had elaborate hairstyles that incoporated flowers and other decorations. Men and women also wore a lot of jewelery, such as earrings, armbands, breastplates, noserings, and anklets. The Hindu male garment was called the dhoti, and the female garment gradually evolved into the sari—a single large cloth draped around the body, with a bodice worn underneath.

When Islam arrived, tailored garments became widespread in northern India. People wore sewn cotton pants called paijama or shalwar, with a long tunic called a kamiz or kurta. For men, turbans became popular. Muslim women were expected to dress modestly, so they began to wear veils, a practice that Hindu women also adopted.

SETTING THE TREND
Bangles, bracelets, and ear studs from the Indus Valley are among the earliest ornaments found in India. They are more than 4,000 years old. The styles of these pieces of jewelery, and the designs on them, were used again in later forms of decoration.

ANCIENT DRESS
A painted fragment of a pillar shows a woman wearing a long red skirt and jewelery. The pillar is about 2,000 years old.

ANCIENT BEAUTY AIDS
This mirror, collyrium applicator, and hair pin are over 4,000 years old. Large, dark eyes were considered a sign of beauty, so women drew attention to their eyes by outlining them with collyrium, a black substance.

MAKE A FLOWER BRACELET

You will need: Half-sheets of thin white card, pencil, scissors, gold paint, paintbrush, half-sheets of white paper, glue, tinfoil candy wrappers, garden wire, pliers.

1 Draw some simple flower shapes on the white card. They should be about ¼ inch in diameter. Give each flower six rounded petals.

2 Cut out each of the flower shapes carefully. Then paint both sides of each flower with gold paint. Leave the flowers to dry.

3 Draw 10 to 12 wedge shapes on the white paper sheets. They should be wider at the bottom than at the top. Cut out the wedge shapes.

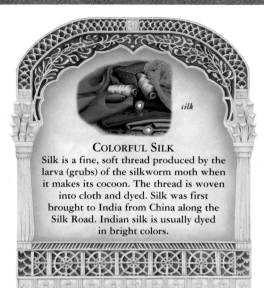

silk

COLORFUL SILK

Silk is a fine, soft thread produced by the larva (grubs) of the silkworm moth when it makes its cocoon. The thread is woven into cloth and dyed. Silk was first brought to India from China along the Silk Road. Indian silk is usually dyed in bright colors.

HINDU DRESS

In this detail from a painted panel, a Hindu man and woman wear typical dress— a dhoti for the man and for the woman, a sari. Both men and women liked to wear bright, colorful clothes.

JEWELS FOR ALL

A Rajasthani woman wears traditional jewelery and dress. Nowadays in India, jewelery is still so valued that even the poorer peasants own pieces for special occasions.

CLOTHING FOR THE COURT

Courtiers from Mughal times wear a side-fastening coat called a jama. It has a tight body, a high waist, and a flared skirt that reaches below the knees. It is worn over tight-fitting pants, or paijama, gathered at the ankle. A sash, called a patuka, is tied at the waist. Courtiers also wore a small turban as a mark of respect.

Floral designs are common patterns used throughout Indian art.

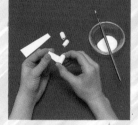

4 Dab glue on the wedge shapes and roll them up to make beads, leaving a hole in the middle. Paint the beads gold, and leave to dry.

5 Carefully cut out tiny circles from the colored tinfoil wrappers. Make sure you have enough to glue to the middle of each flower.

6 Measure a piece of wire long enough to go around your wrist. Add 1 ½ inches for a loop. Tape the flowers to the wire and thread the beads through.

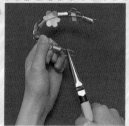

7 To finish the flower bracelet, use a pair of pliers to bend back one end of the wire to form a loop, and the other end to form a hook.

Textiles and Printing

Making textiles has always been an important activity in India. There are records of ancient Romans buying Indian cloth, so the textile trade must have been well established by then. Since fabric does not last very long, there are few examples from before A.D. 900, but sculptures show us the kinds of cotton cloth that were made. In Buddhist and Hindu sculptures, clothing is light and draws attention to the shape of the body.

India's textiles show a lot of different influences. Silk originally came from China, but from about A.D. 100 it was produced in India and became an important Indian export. From about A.D. 1100, Turkish and then Persian invaders introduced floral designs. Fine carpets also began to be made following Persian traditions and styles. Some places began to specialize in the production or sale of textiles. In Mughal times, silks, and muslin (fine cotton fabric) were produced at Ahmedabad, Surat, and Dhaka, and Kanchipuram, near Madras, became famous for its fine silk saris. The Coromandel coast, Gujarat, and Bengal all became textile export centres.

Draped Garment
A red sandstone figure from Jamalpur, from about A.D. 400, shows the Buddha dressed in a fine muslin garment. Many clothes in ancient India were draped and folded instead of being sewn.

Spinning Wheel
A woman sits at her spinning wheel. Weavers were important because Indian fabrics were in great demand in Europe.

Make a Printing Block

You will need: Paper, felt-tipped pen, scissors, raw potato halves, blunt knife, 8 x 6-inch piece of beige calico fabric, iron, scrap paper, paints, paintbrush.

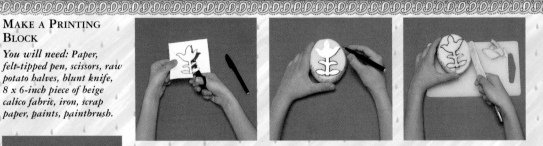

1 Copy the pattern above onto a sheet of paper. You can invent your own Indian design, if you like. Cut out the pattern carefully.

2 Place the cut-out pattern on the cut surface of the potato half. Draw around the outline of the pattern with a felt-tipped pen.

3 Use the knife to cut out the pattern on the potato. Your pattern should be about ¼-inch higher than the rest of the potato half.

PERSIAN-STYLE CARPET

This fine wool carpet is decorated with floral patterns. In Mughal times, many fine carpets like this one were produced in India. Carpet weaving was a skill learned in the northwest of India from Persian craftworkers.

indigo block   madder

RED AND BLUE DYES

Dark-red dyes made from the root of the madder plant, and violet-blue dyes made from the leaves of the indigo plant, were used to dye textiles during Mughal times. Not much is known about the way in which textiles were dyed in earlier times.

PRINTING COTTON CLOTH

A Punjabi man prints a pattern onto a piece of cotton with a printing block. Dyes for cotton cloth were usually made from vegetables.

HUNTING COAT

This satin hunting coat has scenes and animals of the hunt embroidered on it in silk. It is typical of the type of dress worn by Mughal nobles.

Printing blocks were used in Mughal times to decorate fabrics for festivals and other special occasions.

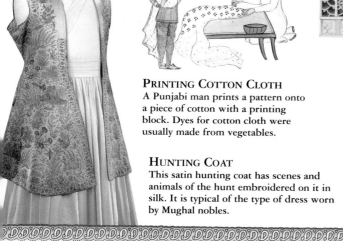

4 Ask an adult to help you to iron the fabric. Lay the ironed fabric on top of scrap paper. Put paint on part of your printing block with a paintbrush.

5 Brush a different color of paint onto your printing block. Give the block an even coat of paint that is not too heavy. Do not drench the block.

6 Press the printing block onto the fabric a few times. When the paint design starts to fade, add more paint to the block with the paintbrush.

7 When the print design has dried, add some colorful details. Try different colors on your printing block, or change the pattern on the fabric.

Gardens

THE GARDENS of the Mughals were enclosed spaces filled with pools and flowering plants. Since they required constant care and watering, gardens were only for wealthy people who could afford servants. Gardeners worked hard to insure that parts of the garden were in bloom all year long. Courtiers amused themselves in gardens by playing games such as hide-and-seek, or with cockfighting. For at least 2,000 years, Indians have been particularly fond of flowers. The mango blossom, ashoka flower, and jasmine all appeared in courtly poetry. The lotus (a kind of water lily), with its underwater stem system and floating flower, was a symbol of goodness and life. Flowers and leaves were used to make garlands to decorate the body and hair, and to decorate images of Hindu gods in the practice of puja (worship).

For Muslims, gardens had a symbolic significance, because they were viewed as a miniature map of paradise. Muslim rulers divided gardens into four parts called charbhags, which were separated by water channels that represented the rivers of paradise. Gardens were so important that they inspired the designs on carpets that were made during Mughal times.

FAVORITE PLANTS
Ponds filled with aquatic plants, such as water lilies, were favorites in both Hindu and Muslim gardens. Courtly poetry describes many varieties of lotus and water lily. Some varieties were grown to bloom at night, by moonlight.

MOUNTAIN GARDEN
A garden, at the mountain fortress of Sigiriya in Sri Lanka, is from c. A.D. 400. It contains the remains of enclosures and pavilions. It once had water works, including fountains, an artificial stream, and a large central tank. Sigiriya is surrounded by a moat. It is said that the moat once had crocodiles in it to deter intruders.

WATERING THE PLANTS
A group of malis (gardeners) use an elaborate system of water courses that intersect at right angles to irrigate plants, in this Mughal period painting.

PARADISE GARDEN

A Persian-influenced carpet is woven with a design inspired by a garden. In Islam, paradise is imagined as a garden that contains the finest objects in the world. Persian carpets were usually woven into designs based on gardens.

TENDING THE GARDEN

Gardens were popular in the houses of rich and powerful people. If a household had no gardener, the women of the house were responsible for tending the garden. Usually, a garden had a mixture of flowers and useful plants, such as fruits and herbs, growing in it.

DANGEROUS PLACE

An intruder pretending to be a gardener is being threatened by the garden's owner, a noble. The painting is from the Mughal period, from the 1600s. In those days, the garden was a place not only of romantic, but also of political intrigue. A powerful person's life could be at risk away from the house.

Weapons and Warfare

FROM ARYAN TIMES, when tribes fought each other and stole each others' cattle, warfare was a fact of life in India. As larger empires came into being, warfare became more elaborate. By the time of the emperor Ashoka in 250 B.C., armies were divided into four parts—infantry (foot soldiers), cavalry (horses), chariots, and elephants. The infantry was the core of all Indian armies, but it was often made up of poorly trained peasants. Elephants, on the other hand, were a symbol of royalty and majesty, and gave an army great prestige.

In the 1000s, when the Turks invaded, chariots became less important. This was because the Turks had excellent horses and could use bows on horseback. Soon, all Indian armies copied them, and began to use high-class cavalry. The first recorded use of gunpowder was in the Deccan plateau, in central India, in the 1400s. Later, the Mughals combined field artillery (guns) with cavalry and elephants.

UNEQUAL CONTEST
A mounted warrior and a foot soldier attack each other. From the 1200s onward, nobles fought on horseback. Foot soldiers faced a great disadvantage in fighting men on horseback, who not only used swords, but bows, too.

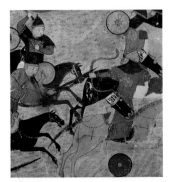

SUPERIOR WARRIOR
A Mongol warrior draws his bow and aims behind him as he rides. The Mongols were great fighters, especially on horseback. In 1398, they devastated Delhi and made many of its citizens slaves.

MUGHAL HELMET

You will need: Strips of newspaper, flour and water or wallpaper paste, bowl, inflated balloon, scissors, fine sandpaper, thin card, Scotch tape or white glue, gold and black paint, paintbrushes, 8 x 4-inch piece of black card, ruler.

1 Soak the newspaper in the paste or flour and water. Cover half of the balloon with three layers of newspaper. Leave to dry between layers.

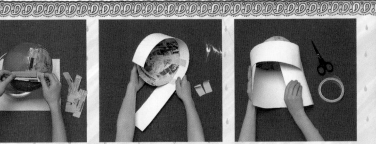

2 When it is dry, pop the balloon and remove it. Sand edges of the helmet with sandpaper. Wrap a strip of card around the base. Tape or glue it.

3 Place a longer piece of card inside the helmet. It should be long enough to cover your ears and neck. Glue or tape it in place, and trim to fit.

LIGHT PROTECTION

A Hindu warrior on horseback uses a spear. Warriors had little armor besides shields. They often wore ornaments and lucky charms.

FORTIFIED CHAIR

A king at war travels in a fortified howdah (chair) on an elephant's back. The combination of the howdah and elephant was like the armored tank of modern warfare. The best army elephants were captured mainly in eastern and southern India, and in Sri Lanka.

BEST WEAPON

A Hindu foot soldier uses a bow and arrows. These weapons, and swords, were the types they preferred. Maces, lances, spears, and daggers were also used.

FINE WEAPONRY

This Mughal dagger handle is inlaid with gold and jewels. Weapons were often crafted from the finest materials.

A Mughal warrior wore a plumed helmet to protect his head during battles.

4 Paint the whole helmet with two coats of gold paint, using a medium-sized paintbrush. Allow the paint to dry completely between coats.

5 Add details with black paint and a fine paintbrush. You could use a Mughal pattern like the one shown above, or design your own.

6 Cut narrow slits ¼ inch apart in the black card. Leave 2 inches uncut at the bottom of the card. Cover this patch with glue, and roll the card up tightly.

7 When the glue is dry, glue the plume to the top of your helmet, or you can cut a small hole in the helmet and push the plume through.

Transportation

TRAVEL IN INDIA hardly changed from the beginning of the country's history until the middle of the 1800s, and journeys were a great deal longer and harder than they are today. Despite the difficulties, people had many reasons to travel and did so quite a lot. They moved from place to place to trade, to go on pilgrimages, or in times of trouble, for example, during wars or famines.

USING THE RIVERS
Boats like this one were used to travel along rivers in the north of India, such as the Ganges. The boats were steered by a large oar, instead of a rudder. Boats were particularly important for people who were traders. Ocean sailing was not a skill that was heavily developed in India.

TRAVEL BY BULLOCK CART
Carts drawn by bullocks or cows were the most common way of transporting humans and heavy loads over long distances, particularly in the countryside. Wheeled carts have been used for 5,000 years, since the time of the Indus Valley civilization.

Most people traveled on foot, and used elephants, pack-oxen, horses, and camels to carry their goods. Wealthier people had servants to carry loads, too. By the time of King Ashoka, around 250 B.C., there was a system of paths crossing plains, mountains, rivers, and other geographical features. These paths had to weave around difficult or inaccessible terrain. During the monsoon, they became very muddy, and sometimes they were even washed away.

To overcome some of these problems, people used the rivers instead. This happened mainly in northern India, since the rivers in southern India were too rocky. Other people traveled up and down the coasts. For over 2,000 years, Indians have been very inventive, and have made many kinds of rafts, floats, and sailing vessels.

A pair of women from Rajasthan, in northern India, carry brass pots stacked on top of each other. They are carrying water from a village well. The pots sit on cloth rings, which protect the crest of the head and provide a neat cavity to hold the bottom of the pot. Bearing loads in India long ago, as today, was done by balancing heavy objects on the shoulders or head. This made it much easier to carry the weights, because the load was spread evenly on the top part of the body.

MONSOON RIVER FLOOD

Mughal forces struggle to ford a stream that has become swollen by the heavy monsoon (wet season) rains. The monsoon season in India made travel difficult. Because of this, Buddhist monks would wander in the hot dry season and settle in monasteries during the rainy season.

TRAVELING BY CHAIR

Trumpeters announce the arrival of a Mughal prince and his wife. The royal couple are traveling in an elaborate chair, called a palanquin. Important people often traveled in these chairs, which were carried on the shoulders of slaves or servants.

THE ADAPTABLE CAMEL

Camels were used for transportation in hot, dry regions, especially in the deserts of Rajasthan and the hills of northwestern India. Camels are well adapted to extremely hot and dry conditions, and they can travel for long periods without water.

Food and Drinks

PEOPLE'S STAPLE (BASIC) FOODS depended on what they could grow. In the wetter areas of eastern, western, southern, and central India, rice was the staple diet. In the drier areas of the north and northwest, people grew wheat and made it into different kinds of breads.

Apart from these staple foods, people's diets depended on their religion. Buddhists thought that killing animals was wrong, so they were vegetarians. Most Hindus, particularly the upper castes, became vegetarians too. Because they believed that the cow was holy, eating beef became taboo (forbidden). When Islam arrived, it brought with it a new set of rules. Muslims are forbidden to eat pork, although they do eat other meat.

The Indians used a lot of spices in their cooking, in order to add flavor and to disguise the taste of rotten meat. Ginger, garlic, turmeric, cinnamon, and cumin were used from early times. Chillis were only introduced from the Americas after the 1500s.

CELESTIAL FRUITS
A heavenly damsel offers fruits in this stucco painting from Sri Lanka. From the earliest times, Indians ate with their hands instead of using implements. Even so, there were rules that had to be followed. Generally, they could only eat with the right hand, being careful to use just their fingers.

EVENING DELIGHTS
A princess enjoys an evening party in the garden. She listens to music by candlelight, and is served drinks, sweets, and other foods.

MAKE A CHICKPEA CURRY
You will need: knife, small onion, 1fl oz vegetable oil, wok or frying pan, wooden spoon, 1½ in piece fresh ginger root, 2 cloves garlic, ¼ tsp turmeric, 1lb tomatoes, ½ lb cooked chickpeas, salt and pepper, 2 tbsp chopped fresh coriander, plus coriander leaves to garnish, 2 tsp garam masala, a lime.

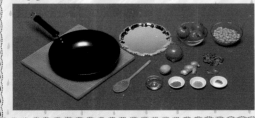

1 Chop the onion finely. Heat the vegetable oil in a wok. Fry the onion in the oil for two or three minutes, until it is soft. Ask an adult to help you.

2 Chop the ginger finely and add to the pan. Chop the garlic cloves and add them, along with the turmeric. Cook gently for another half a minute.

A RICH BANQUET

Babur, the founder of the Mughal Empire in India, enjoys a banquet of exotic fruits. Under the Mughals, a cuisine called Mughlai developed. It became famous for its rich and sophisticated flavors.

turmeric

black mustard seeds   *cardamom*

THREE ESSENTIAL SPICES

Turmeric is ground from a root to give food an earthy flavour and yellow color. Black mustard seed has a smoky, bitter taste. Cardamom—a favorite in northern India—gives a musky, sugary flavor that is suitable for both sweet and savory dishes.

LEAF PLATE

In southern India, banana leaves were (and are still) used as plates for serving and eating food. Southern Indian food uses more coconut than the north, and rice flour is used in several dishes.

DAILY BREAD

Indians eat a variety of baked, griddled, or fried breads, such as these parathas. In much of northern and western India, the staple food is wheat, served in the form of unleavened (flat) breads.

Chickpeas are a popular ingredient in Indian cooking. They have been grown in India for thousands of years.

3 Peel the tomatoes, cut them in half, and remove the seeds. Then chop them roughly and add them to the onion, garlic, and spice mixture.

4 Add the chickpeas. Bring the mixture to boiling point, then simmer gently for 10–15 minutes, until the tomatoes have reduced to a thick paste.

5 Taste the curry, and then add salt and pepper for seasoning, if it is needed. The curry should taste spicy, but not so hot that it burns your mouth.

6 Add the chopped fresh coriander to the curry, along with the garam masala. Garnish with fresh coriander leaves, and serve with slices of lime.

Festivals and Ceremonies

RITUAL CEREMONIES in India go back to Aryan times, when there were fire sacrifices throughout the year. After the growth of Buddhism, the Vedic priests developed a set of rites for important events, such as marriages, caste initiations, and funerals, which Hindus then used for centuries. Many temple festivals developed, too. Some, such as Navaratri and Dasara, honored fierce goddesses. Diwali was a festival of lights in honor of the goddess Lakshmi. In the springtime, people played games at the fertility festival of Holi.

Generally, Muslims had fewer and less elaborate rituals. Islamic festivals included Eid al-Fitr after Ramadan, the month of fasting, and Eid al-Adha, to mark the sacrifice of the lamb by Abraham. Muslims also adopted some of the customs and practices of the Hindus.

HANDY HENNA
Using henna to mark the hands and feet was a common practice in India, and is still part of marriage ceremonies. Henna is a green plant extract that is mixed to a paste with water and used to make patterns on the skin. The paste dyes the skin red.

A FESTIVAL OF FUN
The Vasantotsava (or modern Holi) was a springtime festival of play and courtship. Men and women threw colored powders and squirted colored waters over each other with syringes as they ran through the streets and gardens of the city.

TABLA DRUM

You will need: Very large sheet of heavy card, scissors, measuring tape, pair of compasses, pencil, Scotch tape, newspaper, flour and water or wallpaper paste, bowl, fine sandpaper, calico fabric, bradawl, reddish-brown and blue paint, paintbrushes, darning needle, twine, glue.

1 Cut out a card rectangle 22 x 8 ½ in. Cut slits along both long edges. Use the compasses to measure a card circle with a diameter of 6 ½ in. Cut out the circle.

2 Roll the rectangle to make a cylinder with a diameter of 6 ½ in and tape. Tape the slits so that the drum tapers at each end. Tape the circle to one end.

3 Cover the cylinder with 3 layers of newspaper strips soaked in paste or flour and water. Leave it to dry between layers. Sand the edges with sandpaper.

CEREMONY AROUND THE FIRE

A bride, with her face covered, is led into the marriage pandal (ceremonial awning), which is covered with mango and lime leaves to bring the couple good luck. The bride will follow her husband around the fire. Hindu marriages still take place in the home around a sacrificial fire, and are administered by a Brahmin priest.

END OF FASTING

Muslim men take part in Eid festivities, in Bombay. Muslim men pray in public congregations at a mosque, and give zakat (gifts) to the poor. Then they celebrate with friends and families.

DEATH OF AN IMAM

A passion play with music and drumming is acted out in the streets to celebrate Muharram, the first month of the Muslim calender. For Shia Muslims, the tenth day of Muharram is one of dramatic public mourning to commemorate the death of an imam (spiritual leader) named Husain.

PILGRIMAGE TO MECCA

Muslim pilgrims travel by camel to the city of Mecca, in Arabia (modern Saudi Arabia). Muslims must travel to Mecca once in their lifetime, if it is possible. The journey is called the haj.

The tabla drum was played at ceremonies and festivals.

4 Cut a circle of calico with a diameter of 10 in. Pick holes in the edge with a bradawl. Paint the tabla with two coats of reddish-brown paint.

5 Thread the needle with a long piece of twine and knot it. Place the calico over the tabla's open end. Push the needle and thread through a hole in the calico.

6 Pass the twine across the base and through a hole on the other side of the fabric. Pull the twine tight, to stretch the fabric. Repeat all the way around the tabla.

7 Paint a pattern onto the calico. Then apply a coat of watered down glue. This will help to shrink the calico and pull it tight over the tabla.

Clay and Terra-cotta Crafts

CLAY AND TERRA-COTTA OBJECTS (called ceramics) have played an important part in the study of Indian history, for two reasons. Making ceramics was one of India's earliest crafts. Many objects have been found at archaeological sites, dating as far back as 5000 B.C. and the Indus Valley civilization. Also, because the objects were fired (baked), they have traces of carbon left on them, which has allowed archaeologists to date them very accurately using a process called carbon dating.

In the Indus Valley, people made clay storage jars, terra-cotta seals, and terra-cotta figurines of domestic animals. These clay animals may have been children's toys. People continued to use clay containers throughout India's history. Clay was particularly useful, since it kept things cool in the hot climate. Artists also made terra-cotta figurines of gods and goddesses, though they gradually began to make stone and metal images, too.

RECORD IN CLAY
This terra-cotta cart, found at Mohenjo-Daro, is about 4,000 years old. Figurines like this have been found throughout the Indus valley. Although they were probably only toys, they give us information about the way people lived. For example, we can see that they were already using carts with wheels.

PAINTED POTTERY
A painted gray dish made on the Gangetic plains between 1000 and 500 B.C. Similar pottery was made across the region, which shows that people had contact with each other and shared the same technology.

SIMILAR STYLES
Black and red painted pottery has been found at sites dating from the Indus Valley civilization, and at later sites that date back to around 500 B.C. It is found right across the Indian subcontinent.

MAKE A WATER POT
You will need: inflated balloon, large bowl, strips of newspaper, flour and water or wallpaper paste, scissors, fine sandpaper, strip of corrugated cardboard, Scotch tape, terra-cotta and black paint, paintbrushes, pencil, white glue.

1 Cover the balloon with 4 layers of newspaper soaked in paste. When it dries, cut a slit in it. Remove the balloon. Add layers to taper the top.

2 Roll the corrugated cardboard into a circle to fit onto the narrow end of your water pot to form a base. Stick the base in place with Scotch tape.

3 Cover the corrugated cardboard base with four layers of soaked newspaper. Leave it to dry beween each layer. Sand the edges with sandpaper.

TERRA-COTTA GODDESS

A female terra-cotta figure found in Mathura, Uttar Pradesh. It may be an image of a mother goddess. Many terra-cotta images were made during the Mauryan period (400–200 B.C.) and immediately afterward. They were cheaper versions of the stone sculptures that were built at the imperial court.

bricks

BRICKS FOR BUILDING

In areas of India where stone quarries were less common—and throughout India for more simple homes—clay was baked and made into bricks. Unlike buildings made from stone, structures made from bricks have often not survived the ravages of time.

THROWING A POT

A village potter shapes a clay vessel as it spins on his potter's wheel. Pottery was an important part of the ancient urban and village economies, and is still practiced in India today. Clay used for making pottery is available in most parts of the land.

Clay water pots that are 4,000 years old have been found in the Indus Valley. People carried the pots on their heads.

4 When it is dry, paint the water pot with two coats of terra-cotta paint, to make it look like it is made from terra-cotta. Leave it to dry between coats.

5 Draw some patterns on the water pot with a pencil. Copy the ancient Indian pattern shown above, or create your own individual design.

6 Carefully paint your designs, using black paint and a fine paintbrush. Keep the edges of your lines neat and clean. Leave to dry.

7 Add final details, again using a fine paintbrush. When the paint is dry, seal the surface of the water pot with a coat of watered-down glue

Glossary

A

archaeology The study of ancient remains and ruins.

Aryans A group of people who migrated into India around 1500 B.C.

ascetics Monks or religious wanderers who rejected home life to pursue enlightenment.

B

barter To exchange one item for another, without money.

bodhi tree Symbol of the Buddha. The tree he sat under when he achieved enlightenment.

Brahmi An ancient Indian script.

Brahmins The priests, members of the first caste.

Buddha A prince who abandoned his family to seek enlightenment. Founder of the Buddhist way of life.

C

caste One of four social classes into which Hindus were divided.

chauri A whisk, usually made of yak tail, for fanning flies away.

citadel Fortress near to, or inside a city.

civilization A society that has made advances in art, science, technology, law, or government.

collyrium A black paste used as an eyeliner.

conch A type of large, colorful seashell.

courtier Person attending at a royal court.

cowrie A seashell used as the lowest form of currency near the coastal regions of Ancient India.

D

dargah Shrine to a sufi saint.

deity A god or goddess.

dhoti Traditional Indian dress worn by Hindu men.

discus A heavy disk, the symbol of the god Vishnu.

E

edict Order issued by a king.

Eid al-Fitr Celebration at the end of the month of fasting in Islam.

empire A large number of different lands ruled over by a single person or government.

enlightenment Freedom from ignorance through meditation. Buddhist monks try to achieve enlightenment.

epic Long poem that tells a tale.

F

frieze Decorated border along a wall or ceiling.

G

Ganesha Elephant-headed Hindu god. He is lord of Shiva's armies.

gopuram Gate tower of a southern Indian temple.

gurdwara Sikh place of worship.

H

haj A pilgrimage to Mecca that a Muslim should make at least once.

Hanuman Leader of the monkey army that helps Rama rescue Sita in the *Ramayana*.

Hinduism A religion that includes the worship of several gods and a belief in reincarnation.

Holi A festival of the coming of springtime in ancient India.

hookah Water pipe used to smoke tobacco.

I

incarnation Human form of god.

irrigation Bringing water to dry lands so that crops can be grown.

Islam Religion of Muslim people.

J

jama Side-fastening coat worn with trousers in Mughal times.

jataka A story telling of a previous birth of the Buddha.

K

Kali A fierce form of Shiva's wife.

kangha A comb, one of the five objects carried by Sikh brotherhoods.

Kaurava One of the two feuding families of the *Mahabharata*.

Krishna A Vaishnava god who forms the main character in the *Mahabharata*.

Kshatriya A warrior, a member of the second caste.

M

mace A spiked club used by Hindu warriors.

Mahabharata A story of the contest for succession between the families of the Kauravas and Pandavas.

makara A mythical crocodile-like animal.

mausoleum A very grand tomb.

medieval Relating to the period from about A.D. 500–1500.

minar A tower next to a mosque.

mortar Mixture used to stick bricks or stones together.

mosque A Muslim place of worship.

Muharram First month of the Muslim calender.

Muslim A follower of the prophet Mohammed.

myth An ancient story of gods and heroes.

N

Nagari The modern alphabet of northern Indian languages.

nirvana Freedom from suffering.

O

omen A sign of good or bad fortune in the future.

P

paijama Tight-fitting pants worn during Mughal times.

palanquin A seat or carriage carried on men's shoulders.

Pandava One of the two feuding families of the *Mahabharata*.

paratha A fried wheat bread that is eaten in northern India.

patron Person who gives money and encouragement to the arts.

Persian Language spoken in Persia. It was later used by the Muslim nobility who ruled India.

pilgrim A person who makes a journey to a holy place.

polo A game, similar to hockey, played on horseback.

puja Honoring an icon of a god.

R

Radha A favorite friend of lord Krishna when he was young.

raja Indian king or prince.

Rama The hero-king of the *Ramayana*.

Ramayana The story of Rama's rescue of his wife Sita from the demon Ravana.

Ravana A demon who is the villain of the *Ramayana*.

S

Sanskrit Language of the Aryans. The language of the ruling classes in Ancient India.

sari Traditional female Indian dress.

sceptre A ceremonial staff carried by a king.

Shaivism The belief in Shiva as the lord of the Universe.

shalwar kamiz Long tunic and pants worn in northern India.

Shia A branch of Islam.

shikar A hunting expedition.

Shiva A chief Hindu god.

shrine Sacred place of worship.

Shudra Servant or peasant, a member of the lowest caste.

sitar A guitar-like instrument.

soapstone A soft mineral.

stupa Buddhist place of worship containing a relic of the Buddha.

Sufism Mystical form of Islam.

sultan A Muslim ruler.

T

tabla A drum played in northern Indian classical music.

terra-cotta Reddish-brown unglazed earthenware.

textile Cloth produced by weaving threads together.

turban Headdress worn by Sikh, Muslim, and some Hindu men.

V

Vaishnavism The belief that Vishnu is lord of the Universe.

Vishnu A chief Hindu god.

Veda Ancient Aryan texts.

Vaishya A merchant or farmer, a member of the third caste.

Y

Yaksi A female tree spirit.

Z

zakat Alms that must be given to the poor in Islam.

Index

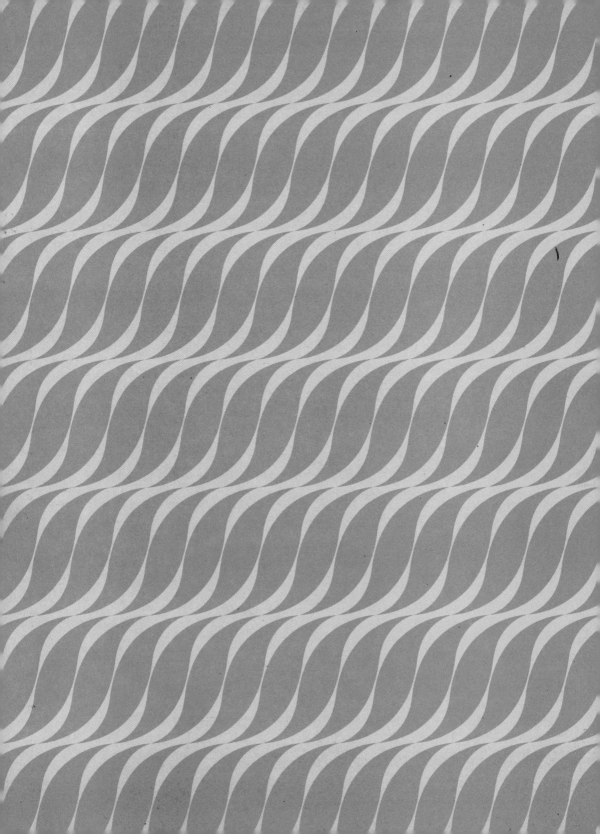